A Good Man To Have In Camp

By John D. Nesbitt:

A Good Man To Have In Camp

John D. Nesbitt

Endeavor Books
Casper, Wyoming

International Standard Book Number 0-892944-01-4

Endeavor Books

7307 6WN Road, Casper, WY 82604
Phone: (307) 265-7410
Fax: (307) 265-3646
Toll Free: (888) 324-9303
E-Mail: endeavorbooks@cwixmail.com

for Laura Stokes

A Good Man To Have In Camp

CHAPTER 1

It reminded him of a brand-new galvanized culvert in miniature, but with more delicate grooves etched inside. The light shining in from the other end made the circles seem, at once, concentric and spiralling. Jim rotated the stock to let the afternoon sun shine right into the chamber, and as he did so he brought into sharp relief the beady point of the firing pin. As he saw the riflings pure and gleaming and bright, he was satisfied.

"Clean as a whistle," he said out loud to himself as he lowered the rifle. He turned it end for end and set it on the table, laying it so that the stock and then the forearm made soft contact with the weathered lumber. The muzzle of the rifle, which an instant before had been aimed into his right eye, now pointed across the back patio towards the bean field.

He took a sip from his gin and tonic. It was a pity, he thought, that people considered gin and tonic to be a summer drink and nothing more. At the moment he was pretty sure he could drink them year around. And he just might.

Since he had moved in, there had not been much of anything urgent to do on the ranch, so for an afternoon he had been content to sit here in the shade of the fruitless mulberry tree, sip on gin and tonic, clean up the guns that had stood so long in the closet, and gaze across the bean field to the oak-peppered foothills beyond. After a couple of gin and tonics on a hot summer day, the world got just a little hazy. Off in the distance the oaks shimmered, and the bean plants in the foreground seemed to sway.

His attention settled on a power pole across the corner of the field on his right. It was about a hundred fifty yards away, he imagined. Back when, before things went sour with Elaine — even before he'd married her — he could have knocked some splinters off that pole. That was a while back, though. He wondered if he still had a good aim, if it was something he could bring back. As he settled his elbows into a rest on the table, the rifle was already in his hands and his cheek was cuddling against the stock. The little bead settled into the notch; he squeezed the trigger. *Click!* he worked the lever and drew another steady bead on the pole. *Click!*

Jim's next sip was the last of that gin and tonic, so he went inside to fix another. Come to think of it, he thought as he squeezed the lime, dry-firing too much like that wasn't supposed to be good for the firing pin. It wouldn't hurt to touch off a shot or two. The .22 magnum made a crack of a noise but not loud, and now that he lived off by himself, he didn't have any close neighbors to worry about. Only open country, sloping back up into the hills, lay beyond the pole, so there was no danger of hitting a house, and he might even land a slug or two in the pole itself.

This time as he settled into position he felt a little thrill run through him. Have to control that heartbeat, he thought. Ruin a good shot. He took a deep breath, exhaled, and brought the sights into line. A movement to the left caught his attention. It was an animal — a mousy grey-brown thing, too big for a dog and too small for a cow. Was it a goat come to poach in the beans? No, it was a deer. It was a slow-moving, browsing deer, working its way in the late afternoon out of the oak trees towards the beans. At that distance Jim couldn't pick up horns, but it didn't matter. Deer weren't even in season yet. He tried bringing the sights to bear on the pole once more, but he found himself lining up on the deer as it walked along the edge of the field. His heartbeat picked up again, and he took another deep breath and exhaled.

Then he felt a familiar tremor run through him, one he had first felt when he was eleven years old. In his uncle's barn he had come across a five-gallon can of tractor grease, a can of greenish-brown goo that had never been opened or dipped into. Its surface was smooth and soft as a bowl of pudding, and it lured him, enticed him, like nothing had ever done before. He felt a surge go through him, a sensation strange and forceful, as he knelt by the bucket. His doubled fist hung for an instant over the perfect surface; then he drew it back and plunged his arm, clear to the elbow, into the bucket of new grease.

He felt it again with the deer. He felt the ancient tingle, the ripple of excitement over a forbidden act. The deer was coming closer with each step until it paused, with its head lifted, a few yards short of the power pole. Jim focused all his attention into the bead and the notch and the target as he pulled the trigger. The gun went *Blap!* Then, to his mixed joy and fear, the deer fell flat on its side.

Jim stood up and walked to the edge of the patio, with the rifle still in his hands. The dark, drab form of the deer was barely visible where it lay in the shimmering green field. The sun struck Jim in the face, hot and dry, so he shaded his eyes and took a broad look, letting the world around him take shape and fill in. He saw no motion and no vehicles, no manufactured colors against the summer tones of the landscape. He was pretty sure no one had seen what he had just done, so he took a minute to put his thoughts in order.

First he put the rifle back in the gun closet, then pitched the gin and tonic, got a long drink of water, and put on a cap. Then he was into the pickup, driving around the field to the spot where the deer had fallen. When he got there he saw it was a young buck — spike on one side and fork on the other — and in less than another month it would have been in season. Jim shook his head at the thought, then grabbed the flopping carcass by the four hooves and hefted it into the back of the truck. As he drove to the barn, he told himself to concentrate on doing a quick, clean job and to be satisfied with the thought that the meat wasn't going to waste.

Backing into the barn, he decided to hoist the deer out of the pickup by tossing a rope over a rafter, tying one end to the deer's legs, and cinching the other end onto the ball hitch of the pickup. By driving forward he could pull the deer up, and later he could let it down by going in reverse.

It might have been a good idea except that the rafters ran parallel to the pickup. He looked around in the junk heaps outside until he found a length of two-inch iron pipe, warm from the afternoon sun. Back inside, he set up a ten-foot ladder and wrestled the pipe onto the rafters, spanning two of them. That was better anyway, he thought. A pipe would give less resistance to the rope.

All this time he had an awareness of the warm deer lying in the back of the hot pickup bed. It gave him a sense of urgency until he told himself that if he did his work carefully, it would take less time in the long run. He tossed the rope up, and it came slithering down over the slick pipe. He caught the loose end, pulled it down, and tied it to the hitch on the bumper. Then he grabbed the deer by the horns and dragged it to the tailgate, looped the other end of the rope over a hock, and flopped the carcass onto the ground. It would be smoother, he decided, to pull it straight up than to have it swing free from the pickup bed.

As he drove forward and saw the deer rise up into view, he nodded.

It all came back to him as he worked — how to dress and skin the animal, how to hold the knife to keep from cutting himself, how to do the tricky part around the brisket. As he got closer to the end of his task, he wondered where he would hang the carcass. The barn was too warm and musty. Out in the yard wouldn't do because it would be too conspicuous. In either place there might be flies, and there was no reason to ruin a good sheet to wrap the carcass, if he was going to cut it up the next day and get the meat into the freezer. Then he thought of the parlor or whatever it was, the large empty room that he fancied would be just right for a pool table. When he had opened the windows the night before, he had felt a nice cool breeze wafting through. And the chandelier hung from the ceiling by a good heavy chain. It should hold the hanging meat, which from the heft of it he imagined would weigh less than sixty pounds.

He found a cotton clothesline rope in the garage, and once inside the house, he poked the rope through a lower link in the chain of the chandelier, then hoisted up the venison. He drew back the drapes and opened the screened windows on either side of the room, stood there a few moments to enjoy the breeze, and then turned off the lights and went to bed.

His first identifiable thought the next morning was that he might not drink gin and tonics every day of the year. As he lay there in bed, with the morning sun streaming in through the window, he remembered events of the evening before. They came in spots, with brief and gentle flashes of horror, but he felt a gradual satisfaction at having made a good shot and having taken care of things in a methodical way. It occurred to him that the morning sun might be warming the meat, and, maybe worse, the drapes were drawn open so that anyone coming in the driveway might see the hanging meat.

The purple carcass was firm and dry, solid as it hung from the chandelier. As he stood there with his hand testing the cool texture of the haunch, his gaze moved towards the driveway and on out to the road. There was a pickup coming up the lane, a dark old pickup that looked like a Ford. It didn't look like the pickup he had seen coming and going when the bean field was being irrigated. Jim pulled the drapes, went back to his bedroom and finished dressing, ran a comb through his hair, and walked out to the driveway to meet his visitor, whoever it might be.

The pickup was creeping along, presumably to avoid raising too much dust. Jim crossed the barnyard and went into the little shop that was built onto the end of the barn. The day before, he had decided to replace a cracked handle on the clamshell posthole digger, so he now took a box-end wrench off the pegboard and went to work on the digger. From his vantage point he heard the rattle of the pickup and saw the visitor drive into the yard. The man parked under the sycamore tree, rolled a cigarette and lit it, and got out. As he crossed the yard he pulled on the brim of his straw hat; at the shop door he stopped and took a drag on his cigarette.

Jim felt the man's gaze and looked up. He took a quick impression of the stranger, who was dressed in field boots, worn blue jeans, and a short-sleeved chambray shirt. The straw hat was of a western variety, a grade above the common field hat sold for a couple of dollars in a supermarket, but still the color of straw — not the dressier type of tight-woven, hard-shelled white hat that the cowboys wore to rodeos and dances. The man had pale blue eyes and a rough complexion; he was clean-shaven but looked like he needed a haircut, as his light brown hair poked over the tops of his ears. The ears themselves stood out, as in the old joke about a Chevy coupe with the doors open. Jim was about to ask what he could do for him when the stranger spoke.

"You Jim Lander?"

"Sure am."

"Folks in town said you could maybe use a hand for a while."

"Which folks?"

6

"Folks in a little bar called the No-Tell."

"They should know. They know most of what goes on around these parts." Jim raised his eyebrows and turned down the corners of his mouth.

"So I thought I might take a drive out here and see if you got any work for the next little while."

Jim glanced at the stranger. "How long you looking for work?"

"At least a month, longer if things work out right."

"I could use a hand, that's for sure. I got quite a bit of work to do around here to get this place into shape." Jim waved his wrench at the farmyard. "It's been left to sort of gradually run down the last few years, and I'm taking it over and trying to pick it back up."

The stranger nodded as if he'd had a look on the way in, then took a drag on his cigarette.

Jim went on. "I'm waiting right now — been waiting — to get the final word from the bank. And a check so I can operate. I'm supposed to know by Tuesday."

"Today's Saturday."

"Yeah." Jim paused with the wrench and then rapped it to knock dried mud from the digger. "I'll tell you, though, I don't have much ass-sittin' work. I hope you don't mind taking the business end of a shovel or hoe." Jim glanced up.

The pale blue eyes met him. "I got plenty of that left in me."

"See, I got that farmland down on the flat leased out, or the bank did, so it's not mine right now. Same with the bean field in the back, too. But we got hoeing and clean-up to do on this permanent pasture back here, to bring it back around, and I've got a lot of fence to build and mend."

"That's fine. You got cows here?"

"Not yet. A while back I sold a dairy down in the valley, and I'm just getting settled here. And to tell you the truth, after nine years of milk cows day in and day out, I don't mind getting settled in gradually. But I have a lot to do."

The stranger nodded as if he'd heard some of it before. He took a long drag on his Bull Durham, then dropped the snipe on the cement floor and snuffed it out with his boot. As the man lowered his head, Jim noticed he had a prominent, narrow nose to match the wide ears.

The stranger looked up and said, "Any place to stay here?"

Jim stepped out of the shop and used the wrench to point across the yard. "There's a little cabin-type affair over there, the shack with the tin roof, and it's got a shower and sink and lights. We can rig you up a little hot plate if you want." The newcomer squinted in the direction of the shack, and Jim went on. "It's mostly been used for storage — for fertilizer and tools and that — but we can clear it out for you."

"We'll take a look at it," the man said, and walked away.

Jim went back to loosening the bolts on the digger handle. After a few minutes he heard the other man come crunching back across the barnyard.

"It'll do," the man said. "Shower works."

Jim squinted. "We'll probably have to do something about a refrigerator before long, too, then."

"I got an ice box I can use for the time bein'."

"I'll see about rounding up a refrigerator."

The man made a noise with his mouth and then spoke. "Start work when?"

"Oh, um, let's see. I won't have the real go-ahead till Tuesday, but I guess we can start Monday. Give you the weekend to get the place liveable."

"I'll go back into town, get my stuff, and get started on it this afternoon. Shall I put all that stuff that's in there in the barn?"

Jim pushed out his lower lip. "I can give you a hand with it."

"Nah, I'll get it. Barn all right?"

"Sure. We'll need to check the water heater, too."

"I'll do that."

The man's quickness made Jim pause before he said, "Well, okay. I'll go out and see about a refrigerator. And by the way, what's your name? I'll need your social security number, too, but no hurry about that."

"Name's Brant. Harold Brant."

"Good to meet you, Harold." They shook.

"Real fine, Jim. We'll see you later on." Brant crunched back over to his pickup, rolled another cigarette, gunned up the Ford, and rattled out just as he had rattled in.

Jim went back to the posthole digger and finished taking out the cracked handle. He recalled what the old man had told him about the kind of man who smoked Bull Durham and wore a straw hat: never hire one. And now he'd gone and done it, even invited him to move in. The guy was a little forward, like he might have a mind to do things his own way once in a while. That wasn't why a fellow wasn't supposed to hire that type, though. The reason was that the man would spend all his time rolling cigarettes and chasing his straw hat, and not get any work done. It was sort of a joke with the old man, about a class of people, and he'd usually tell the joke when money was a little close and he was smoking roll-your-owns himself. Jim had a flash of the old man rolling a cigarette and licking it, and he smiled. The old man might have been amused at this. Well, he'd done it, anyway.

He went in and made coffee, then came out with a cup and finished replacing the digger handle. By the time he'd set the water on the apricot tree and knocked down a few weeds, it was lunch time. The hired man, Brant, wasn't back yet, but there wasn't anything Jim couldn't do by himself. Then he remembered the refrigerator. Today was

Saturday, so it might be a good time to drop by Ernie's. He might know something about a refrigerator, or feel like poking around looking for one.

CHAPTER 2

Jim drove to town seven miles, then north two more to Ernie's place, where Ernie and his wife Brenda lived on a snug little two-acre place. Ernie had it pieced up into smaller parcels where he kept a beef or two, a couple of lambs, a vegetable garden, and a family orchard that at one time might have been productive. As he pulled into the driveway, Jim could see Ernie watering the garden and drinking a bottle of Budweiser. Jim shut off the engine, pulled the brake on the pickup, and got out.

Ernie hoisted his beer in the air and pointed to the house, as if to tell Jim to get himself one on the way out. Jim did. He did not see Brenda in the house, and since her car had not been in front, he imagined she was out somewhere.

Ernie was watering the okra and jabbing the ground with a shovel. His light brown, wavy hair stuck out from beneath his cap, and his blue eyes shined as he looked at Jim. "What's new today?"

"Not much. Looking to buy a refrigerator."

"New one?"

"Nah, old one."

"What for? Your barn?"

"I need one for my hired man's cabin."

"Hired man?" Ernie gave him a close look.

"Yeah, I hired me a man who smokes Bull Durham and wears a straw hat. Came out looking for about a month's work or so, and I said I could put him to work come Monday."

"How much you paying him?"

"By golly, we never talked about that."

"You probably will."

Jim thought about Brant and how he seemed. He smiled and said, "Yeah, I'm sure we'll talk about it."

Ernie tilted his head. "Best place I know to get a refrigerator is that second-hand store on the old highway south of town."

"You feel like running out there when you get done here?"

"Sure, I wouldn't mind rummaging around there a little bit. Smokes Bull Durham and wears a straw hat, uh?" Ernie smiled. "What would your old man say about that?"

"I thought about it."

"Here." Ernie handed him the shovel. "Why don't you watch the water for me for a minute while I go take a leak and get another beer. You ready for one?"

Jim looked at his, took a guzzle, and said, "I will be by the time you get back."

On the way out to the ranch, with the refrigerator in the back of the pickup, Jim decided to tell Ernie about the deer. "That .22 magnum of mine is still sighted in pretty well."

Ernie tipped his beer. "Is that right?"

"Sure is. I shot a young buck right in the noggin from my back patio yesterday. He was across the corner of the bean field there, maybe a hundred and fifty yards."

Ernie looked around. "The hell you did."

"Yeah, right in the head. Surprised the hell out of me."

"Him, too, I bet. Nice buck?"

"Yeah, young one with a spike on one side and a fork on the other."

Ernie smiled. "So you were just shittin' me about the guy with the Bull Durham and the straw hat."

"What do you mean?"

"You're gettin' this refrigerator to store your venison in, looks like."

Jim shook his head. "No, this is for my hired man. I'm gonna cut up the meat this evening. You can help."

"Brenda and I are going out this evening. Cut it up in the morning, and I'll help you. Will it keep? Where you got it?"

"I got it hanging in that big empty room in front, where I want to put in a pool table. We'll take a look at it."

Ernie gave a half-frown. "Your hired man know about it?"

"None of his damn business."

"That's what I'd say." With a flourish Ernie twisted the top off of a beer. "You ready?"

Jim drained his and tossed it at Ernie's feet, geared down to turn in to the driveway of the ranch, and said, "Yep."

Brant was sweeping out the shack when Jim and Ernie pulled up. He announced right away that he had gotten the water heater fired up. Jim and Ernie unloaded the refrigerator, and then after Jim made introductions, he and Ernie went into the house, leaving Brant to his work.

Jim asked, "So what do you think of my hired man?"

"About like you said. Let's look at that deer meat."

Ernie touched the meat here and there, stuck his nose inside the rib cage and sniffed. "Yeah, hell yes. Just open the windows tonight, and it'll keep fine. We can cut it up in the morning. You had the windows open last night, I imagine."

"Yeah. But I'd just as soon leave the front window closed. I don't know this guy all that well yet." He twisted his mouth and thought for a second. "Maybe I can leave the window open and the drapes pulled in front."

"That might work all right." Ernie patted the loin. "Nice piece of meat there, Jim."

Jim looked at his watch. "I probably ought to be getting you back to your place if you got your chores to do and want to go out this evening."

"Yeah, probably ought to."

Jim sat in the Buckhorn Bar after leaving Ernie off at his place. He drank slowly on his beer, eyeing the pay phone and wondering if he should call Dusty. He hadn't known her all that long to be calling her on short notice, but she didn't seem to stand on ceremony. They had gone to the county fair together, and aside from having bumped into Elaine and her new escort, the evening had gone off without much discomfort, and he had told Dusty he would call her.

As he sat at the bar with his beer, he had a pleasant image of her. She had been wearing denim shorts and a pale green blouse, both of which set off her tan nicely. Her face was clear, not gobbed with makeup, and it didn't have any wrinkles or crow's feet yet. The expression in her clear hazel eyes showed thought. Setting off the face was a full head of what some people would call dishwater blonde hair — it was between blonde and light brown, and it was what had fetched her the name of Dusty. Jim liked the name, thought it was an improvement on what she had started out with — Vernita. Vernita Woodson. Dusty Woodson now.

As he thought about it, he liked everything about her — her build, her appearance, her expression, her touch. If he felt uncomfortable at all, as he sometimes did, it was because she was eight years younger. That's why she had a youthful face: she was only twenty-three.

She seemed plenty grown-up in the way she handled her personal life. She didn't play the games he had been through with some of the other young women he had met — being coy, stringing him along with a maybe, wondering out loud what he thought of her. If he asked Dusty to do something like go out, she would say yes or no without making it into an elaborated tease. That's why he thought he might call her on short notice.

He knew he should have called earlier in the week, but he had been hesitant then. Now he wasn't — partly because he'd had a few beers to cut the nervousness, and partly because he just wanted to see her.

He went to the pay phone and called her number.

Tammy, her roommate, answered. "She's not here. Can I ask who's calling?"

"Jim Lander."

"She's still at work, Jim. You can catch her there."

"Okay. Thanks, Tammy." Well, if she was working, maybe he would eat dinner in town. She might wait on his table or at least drop by long enough for him to put in a question.

The Westside Lodge was a decent, middle-priced motel with a coffee shop and dining room. The motel itself made its living off of freeway trade, while the restaurant catered to travelers and townsfolk alike — people whose idea of going out for dinner was chicken-fried steak or low-calorie plate. It was a decent place all the same, and a fellow didn't have to worry if he came in unscrubbed from the field.

He took a small table by the partition, sipped on his ice water, and said, yes, he'd have coffee. A woman in a modified beehive, a woman about forty who reminded Jim of those motherly old milk cows that had had about half a dozen calves, took his order.

He hadn't hit the seating quite right, but he caught Dusty's eye. She came over as he was finishing his salad. She looked fine in the plain white blouse and black skirt that the Westside waitresses wore.

"Oh, hi, Dusty. Tammy said you were working, so I thought I'd stop in."

"What did you order?"

"Pork chops."

"Good. I was going to warn you away from the chicken à la king."

"No danger there."

She tapped her pen on her pad, and the silence hung for a moment. Then she went to turn away, saying, "Well, I hope you enjoy your meal . . ."

"Dusty," he said, in a low voice.

15

She held in place. "Yes?" She looked at him, answering with her eyes.

"I was thinking of coming back into town, maybe have a drink or so at the Blue Flame. Would you have time later on?"

She gave a small twist to her mouth. "I get off work at ten. I could probably meet you at ten-thirty or eleven." The hazel eyes held him, then let him go.

"That would be fine," he said. "I'll look forward to it."

"Me too."

He met up with Ernie and Brenda at the Blue Flame, so he sat at their table as he waited for Dusty. Ernie had cleaned up and was no longer wearing a cap. Brenda's solid brown hair looked rich and glossy as it touched her shoulders. They looked like a natural couple, both blue-eyed and smiling.

"Ernie says you hired yourself a hand," Brenda said.

"Yeah, I think he might work out all right."

Ernie joined in. "I told Brenda if she rode out with me in the morning she could get a look at him and judge for herself."

Jim looked at Ernie and back at Brenda. "Ernie told you about my other little escapade?"

Brenda smiled. "Yeah," she said. "I'll help wrap."

"What time you think you'll be coming out?" Jim asked.

"Not too early," Ernie answered. "Maybe nine or so. Or is that too early for you? You out howlin' at the moon tonight?"

"No, not exactly. I'm supposed to meet that girl Dusty here when she gets off work in a little while."

Brenda stirred her Tom Collins. "Is that the girl who works at the Westside?"

"Uh-huh."

"Well, good," she said. "Be sure she sits with us."

"You bet," Ernie said. He smiled and wrinkled his nose, then patted Brenda on the leg.

Dusty got there in time to have a few drinks and a few dances. She was also there long enough for Ernie and Brenda to invite her and Jim to go on a camping trip with them. Jim felt himself squirm. Dusty said it depended on her work schedule. Ernie said he would by God talk to the manager, that they all needed a weekend to get out of this damned valley heat and get up to the mountains and sit in the shade and watch the water flow. Dusty said, without a great deal of commitment that Jim could notice, that it sounded like fun. Brenda asked Ernie to dance.

When the music stopped after last call and the lights came on, Ernie and Brenda got up first to leave. "We'll see you about ten or so in the morning, then," Ernie said, as he shucked a dollar onto the table for a tip.

"Sure. Ten o'clock is fine," Jim answered, and as he watched them walk away he wondered if it was Brenda's idea or Ernie's to show up at that hour.

He turned to Dusty. "Well, what do you think?"

"About what?"

"About what to do now. Are you interested in breakfast?"

"Not really. I had to work that shift last week, and I got enough of the drunks. I was glad to work dinner this weekend."

He hesitated, then went ahead. "How would you like to watch the lights twinkle from up on the hill?"

She paused. "That might be all right," she said, "but I think some other time might be better."

Jim felt himself retreating, as if he had overstepped. Then he saw a soft look in her eyes and felt reassured. "It's a nice view," he said, "up and away from town. At night you can see all the lights of town. I hope you get to see it some time."

She smiled. "I hope so, too."

Jim walked her to her car, kissed her once, and drove home. The seven miles flowed by, and he turned into the ranch and drove up the hill to the house. As he pulled into the yard, his headlights swung around on Brant's blue-black pickup. The bracket holding on the license plate had the name of a car dealer, which Jim didn't read in the sweep of the headlights, and the word "Bakersfield" in capital letters, which Jim recognized from earlier in the day. He thought, even if Brant had brought a girl home with him, it was his own business. Jim put his pickup in reverse, then pulled it around and parked it so he could look down on the valley. The lights of town gave him a sure feeling, that things were safe and orderly and stable. Somewhere under those lights, Dusty was going to sleep. He imagined Elaine was down there, too.

He let out a short, heavy breath, got out of the pickup, and went into the house.

Jim had toast and coffee for breakfast and had begun sharpening knives when Brenda and Ernie pulled in. Ernie sniffed as he came into the kitchen and then went into the next room to look at the meat. When he came back, he and Brenda got organized at the kitchen counter, setting out the cutting boards, wrapping paper, and tape.

Jim boned the meat, Ernie cut and trimmed it, and Brenda wrapped it in small, firm packages. A coastal blacktail was a small deer, yielding thirty or forty pounds of meat, but when it was processed this way, it was all good, clean meat, lean and rich-tasting.

As the pile of bones grew, Jim said, "If you find a polite way to get these out to the car, and a discreet way to feed them to Sam without bringing down the law, I won't have to worry about where to dump them."

Ernie gave a little laugh. "My thoughts, too."

Sam was a Golden Retriever that had a pretty good life. Brenda and Ernie had been married for six years and hadn't had any kids yet, so Sam got preferential treatment. He had his own rug and a basket of toys, and anyone who went to visit Brenda and Ernie got to know Sam. Jim had noticed that some people made a face when Brenda let Sam lick a plate or skillet, but Jim wasn't troubled. He had always liked dogs. Elaine hadn't, so he had phased out of having one for himself. He liked Sam, and now it was a pleasure to send him some scraps.

When they finished the work, Jim convinced Ernie and Brenda to take a few packages for themselves. Then, when they had gone and Jim had the meat stacked in the freezer, he was by himself again. With nothing doing in town, and Dusty working the lunch shift on Sunday, he decided to take a drive up the back side of the ranch, along the hills.

He parked in the shade of a big oak, with the nose of the old Chevy poked towards the valley. This spot was higher than the parking place in front of the house, so he had a wide, hazy view of the fields stretched out patchworklike below him. It was restful up here, the first real rest it seemed he'd had in nine years.

Life had been too tight, too bordered. It was milk the cows at three in the morning, milk the cows at three in the afternoon, worry about the hay, worry about the green chop, worry about the butterfat, milk the cows in the morning, and around and around. Those damn milk cows never knew a day off or a holiday or a hunting season. They were there twice a day, every day.

Being married to Elaine had been like being tied down to the dairy. She never eased up. It wasn't that she bitched or whined for him to make more money, but there was always that next little something she wanted. She had to live in town in the first place, and then she always had her eye on a better appliance or piece of furniture that would set things off just so. Her view of life also included a new car every four years, and then it began to broaden further. She seemed determined to put in a swimming pool. They argued about it and then

19

didn't talk about it, and before they ever resolved the problem, Jim moved out. The swimming pool was the issue that had pushed them over the edge, but it wasn't the whole reason for the divorce. The real reason, as Jim saw it, was pressure — the constant push to live a life that he didn't choose. For him, that meant he had to worry about the hay, worry about the green chop, worry about the butterfat.

Well, that was down there now, and she could do the worrying and planning and acquiring with someone else. Jim imagined her walking out of the trim, remodeled home in town, swaying her trim little ass out to the carport, scooting into the trim little Audi they'd bought, and humming off to her trim little job at the county clerk's office.

"She can have it," he said out loud, with a wave of the hand towards town. She could. Life wasn't so damned tight up here.

And as for women — well, he'd been out with one the night before, so he wasn't exactly a loser.

He looked around at the land below him. There was a lot of work to be done, but life was his at least. He was getting back on his feet, and this was his little empire, to run as he damn well pleased. His thoughts went back to the house and yard. He remembered he had to line up a day's work for the hired man, so he cranked up the pickup and rumbled out of the shade of the oak to take a closer look at what needed to be done on the empire.

CHAPTER 3

While Brant cleaned out the irrigation ditch to the permanent pasture on the upper flat, Jim dug up two sturdy young
oak trees from along the fringe of the foothills and hauled
them, along with a load of corral compost, to the front gate.
He intended to plant one on either side of the entry.

The ground was hard clay, as he knew it would be, and he
punched hard with the digging bar. When it was time for the
shovel he tossed the bar into the shade of the pickup, where
he had also set the trees. He smiled as he thought that someday, if things went well with the little fellows, he and his
pickup would sit in their shade.

As he imagined the twin oak trees growing and spreading,
he recalled a story from high school. One of the older Silva boys,
Tony, had a big hot Pontiac GTO, which he had painted a Portagee
yellow and which everyone called his Portagee Cadillac. It was
a conspicuous car, and after he'd been seen out by the rock quarry
a few times, people took to razzing him and his girl friend. So he
started finding new places to park, and one night he was parked
beneath a couple of oaks at a roadside rest on the old highway,
and a big branch came crashing down on the hood of his car. The
people who had been calling him Rock Pile now began calling
him Shady Rest. Jim smiled at the thought that on some future
night, twenty years from now, some young couple might pull in
under the cover of these two trees.

By lunch time he had the young oaks planted and watered in
a good soil mix. When he drove back to the house, Brant's pickup
was in the yard. It was parked where Jim liked to park his at this
time of day — in the shade of the sycamore tree. Jim squeezed his
pickup next to the other one and went into the house to eat.

While he was munching a tuna fish sandwich and listening to the noontime news, the telephone rang.

21

"Jim? This is Brenda."

"Oh, hi. What's up? Let me turn down the radio, okay?"

"Ernie said you were interested in getting a horse."

"I've thought about it, but I think I'm going to have to wait a while."

"This is one of those deals where you get to keep the horse for someone else. You feed it and keep it, and you get to ride it."

"What kind of horse?"

"The ad says Appaloosa mare, seven years old."

"Is that in today's paper?"

"Uh-huh."

"Are you calling from work?"

"Yeah. I'm on lunch break, and I came across this ad, so I thought I'd give you a call."

"I'm glad you did. I suppose I'd better look into it. Can you read me the number?" He copied it down. "That's a local number, isn't it?"

"Yes, it is. It's a local number."

"Well, I'd better check into it. Thanks a bunch, Brenda."

"Any time. Good luck."

Jim called the number and spoke with a pleasant-sounding woman, who said the horse's name was Babe. She described the horse as blue-grey and not very big. She and her husband had bought the horse for their teen-age daughter, who had fallen in love with Babe because the horse "looked so different." The daughter had ridden Babe for a few months and then lost interest, and now she was all caught up in cheerleading. The parents, prune growers who lived fifteen miles southeast of town along the river, had decided to farm out the horse with an option to buy.

Getting a little further into details, Jim gathered that the people wanted to get rid of the horse, even though it was not a financial burden. The woman said they had a saddle and other tack to go along with the horse. They would like to sell those things, and they would be willing to work out a deal on payments. Jim hesitated, saying he didn't even know how he would get the horse to his place. The woman said they had a neighbor who would lend a horse trailer. Jim said he would think it over and call her back if he was still interested.

After lunch, Jim asked Brant what he knew about horses.

"Some. About as much as I want to."

"Well, I've got a deal I could make on one."

Brant shrugged. "That's up to you."

"Yeah, I know. But I don't know much about 'em. I haven't had a horse before. Just a lot of milk cows."

"Well, they're a pain in the ass, if you ask me. They're tempermental, to begin with. You gotta take care of 'em twice a day, just like your milk cows, unless you just want to turn 'em out to pasture, and you always got vet bills on top of it all."

"This one's a mare."

Brant wrinkled his nose. "That much worse. They come into heat all the time."

"Is that bad?"

Brant gave him a knowing look. "They're like a whore. Always wantin' it."

"Hmm." Jim wondered how much the man knew about whores, if that was what he thought about them.

Brant went on. "They don't settle down, and they stir up any other horse you got around."

Jim nodded, not in agreement but to avoid disagreement. He wondered if the man knew any more about horses than he did about whores. Then he settled on one thing Brant said that made a difference. A horse would be a daily commitment, like milk cows. In that moment, Jim decided he didn't want to take on that much bother for a while. "I think I'll wait," he said.

Brant shrugged and took out the makings for a smoke. "Didn't mean to talk you out of it."

"No, you didn't. I just needed to think out loud about it."

Brant went about his work of cleaning out the ditch without complaint or comment. It was a cement ditch that hadn't been cleaned in several years. It had layers of caked silt in the bottom, with weeds growing all along the bottom and in any cracks or seams up along the side. Jim had explained to Brant that he would have to clean the ditch, cut any good-sized weeds along the edges, and shape up the banks on either side to give support to the concrete. He told Brant he could do those things in whatever order he chose, and Brant decided to clean the inside first. Jim imagined that if he were doing it himself, he would have cleaned and shaped the banks first and then thrown all the dirt and weeds on top. But he supposed the hired man wanted to get the most miserable part done first, so he said nothing. If Brant wanted to hoe star thistles through a layer of junk, that was up to him.

The next day, when Jim got the go-ahead from the bank, he looked over his budget and worked out a new one based on how he really wanted to do things. His idea was to lease out the irrigated crop land for another year and then to put some of it into alfalfa and some of it into permanent pasture. In the meanwhile, he needed to concentrate on fences — around the upper pasture first, and then around the other fields. If he had the place in shape by fall, he would be ready for cattle for the winter. If prices were good he could buy his own, and if prices were not so good, he could lease the pasture and break even.

He spent some time looking over the fences and making a list, and on Thursday and Friday he made trips to town to buy fencing supplies. As he drove back and forth, he noticed the way one fellow was mowing a walnut orchard. The driver was a young man — a year or two out of high school, from the looks of him. He was driving a blue Ford tractor and pulling a red mower, the older kind with an offset tongue that required the driver to turn always to the left. Once a driver would cut out a pattern he would stick to it, as this kid was doing. He would go up the orchard with a row of trees on the left, turn left and cross back one row, make another pass with the trees on his left, come out at the end by the road, turn left and go two rows, turn in, and continue the pattern. Going up the orchard he was always a row ahead of where he was coming back, and the walnut trees were spaced far enough apart that he left an uncut swath in the middle between rows. It was a large orchard, so there were rows and rows of uncut middles.

Jim smiled. He had done the same thing, on a different farm, when he was that age. He had saved the middles for three days in a row, sticking to the harder work of mowing next to the trees. Then he had gone to a party at the river and had stayed out late, assuming he had an easy day ahead of him. When he got to work the next morning, the boss told him he was going to break in a new tractor driver on that whole field of middles. He put Jim to work disking in a prune orchard, where the low branches with green fruit slapped him in the face as he kept his eye on the tree trunks.

Whenever he was mowing after that, he took it easy at the end of each day and cut the middles he had saved up that day. Maybe this kid here would learn the same thing — take the easy parts when you could get them.

Jim had stayed on that job all through the summer and fall, and then when the prunes and walnuts were all in and the wet weather came on, he was out of a job. That was another lesson that a fellow took seriously if he learned it for himself. Being out of a job and living from paycheck to paycheck left him feeling empty when the cold, drizzly weather set in. He tried to get on in the warehouses and packing plants, but he had no luck, so he found a job milking cows.

There were no layoffs with Vern Peterson — quite the opposite. Vern was the type who would sit in the bar and let his wife and daughters milk the cows. Jim had known the two girls in school, and they had always expressed embarrassment at having to milk cows. When the two girls were grown up and gone, Vern's wife left. Vern hung on for a couple of more years, using Jim to get most of the work done. He could never pay Jim in full, so by the time he was ready to sell out, he would have had a sizeable labor claim against him. So he offered the place to Jim, traded back wages for part of the down payment, took what little he could get on top of that, and left town for good.

Jim's dad helped him put up some of the rest of the money for the down. "He could have stiffed you on your wages," he said, "but he had a little pride left, even if he'd pissed away just about everything else. And he got out when he could."

The old man was right. He also said it was harder than it used to be for a fellow to get a start on his own. He said that even if Jim wasn't crazy about milking cows, at least he had a start. Jim could see that, too. Most fellows his age who worked their own places had gotten a start with their families.

Then Jim was on his own and had to make a go of it, at a time when the little dairies were either going out of business or getting bigger. Anyone who still dumped milk into a milk can instead of having a pipeline and a tank was going to end up broke. Jim went into it up to his ears, worked both milkings every day, and did the rest of the work in between. He met Elaine, which put him out of any danger of ever sitting in the bar and leaving his wife to milk the cows, and life was pretty well cut out for him. From then on, there hadn't been any middles.

On his trip into town on Friday morning, he called Dusty. He could just as well have called from home, but when he was in town he felt closer to her.

Her voice sounded tired as she answered the phone with a mumbled "Hello."

"Hi, Dusty. This is Jim. Sorry if I woke you up."

"That's all right. They've got me working graveyard again, that's all."

"Are you working that shift for the whole weekend?"

"Friday and Saturday I am. Then I have Sunday off."

"Well, I should let you get back to sleep. Shall I call back on Sunday afternoon?"

"That would be fine."

"Okay. Sorry to bother you."

"It's all right. Thanks for calling."

"Bye."

Jim got back to the ranch in time for lunch, kept himself busy through the afternoon, and went about his evening routine of getting cleaned up, fixing dinner, and washing dishes. Then it was nine o'clock on a Friday evening, and he had the feeling of an empty weekend stretching out ahead of him. People would be starting to go downtown now, laughing and talking and listening to music. In his mind he could see them, people from town and people from the country, coming together. In the crowd he saw women with purses slung over their shoulders, women with long hair and smiling eyes, women in blue jeans, women in shorts.

Brant had already left, no doubt to cash his paycheck and spend at least some of it. Jim liked the feel of the place better when Brant wasn't around, but he still felt the itch to go to town, to mix with the music and laughter. After a little more fidgeting he turned off the lights, went out to his pickup, and started for town.

As he drove out of the yard he could see it was a clear night across the valley, and when he was down on the flat he saw the full moon through the windshield of the pickup. No wonder the night was so bright, with such a large, brilliant moon. He raised his eyebrows. People said a full moon brought out the animal in a man. Maybe that was why he felt restless. As he drove on, his headlights caught a pair of blue eyes at the edge of an alfalfa field. Deer eyes. Poacher's moon, that's what it was. It brought out the night life.

He headed for the Trail's End, the honky-tonk bar in town. It was the place where people went to meet, get rowdy, or

27

merge with the crowd. The No-Tell, the Buckhorn, and a couple of others like them were small bars with juke box music — places that had their regular customers, happy hour specials, free-food nights, football pools, and sloppy drunks.

A model of politeness by comparison, the Blue Flame had a lounge atmosphere with live music, plenty of small, round tables with candles, and cocktail waitresses who had husbands. If the No-Tell occupied one end of the scale and the Blue Flame the other, the Trail's End plunked itself down somewhere in the middle.

The Trail's End might seem low-brow to folks who had never had any cowshit on their boots, but it had one claim to sophistication: the apostrophe in its name. At the other end of the valley, nearly a hundred miles away, another honky-tonk operated under the same name. As the story went, the owners of the other place had declared, a few years earlier, that they were going to sue for the exclusive right to put the name on matchbooks and napkins, since they had had the name first. The owners of the local Trail's End bluffed them down. They pointed out that the other bar did not have an apostrophe on its sign, so the meaning was different. "Trails End" without the apostrophe was a complete statement, a subject and a verb, whether the owners knew it or not. With the apostrophe, it meant the end of the trail, just an adjective and a noun. No more came of the threat from farther south, but the incident became part of local lore. When a patron wrote a check, there was usually someone sure to holler, "Don't forget the damn apostrophe!"

Jim, who had been brow-beaten on the use of the apostrophe when he was in school, liked the place well enough.

He made it to the Trail's End in time to get a seat at the bar. He knew most of the people in the place, including Dusty's roommate, Tammy. Jim sent a drink her way, and she came by to thank him for it. She was a year or two younger than

Dusty, not much past the minimum age of twenty-one. She had shoulder-length blonde hair and a full figure, which Jim admired as she walked away. She was appealing, but maybe a little too young even if she hadn't been Dusty's roommate, so Jim did not find it hard to stay in line.

Things changed by the time he was drinking his second beer. He saw a brown head of hair move through the crowd, and as he registered the partial recognition he felt a surge run through him. Then he got a better look; it was sure enough Arlene. He felt himself start to tingle, and he kept looking her way until he caught her eye. He turned halfway from the bar as she came over to stand next to his stool.

Jim knew for a fact that she was four or five years older than he was, but she didn't look it. She wore her brown hair cut and combed back like the younger women and under-age girls, and her face was smooth. Tonight she was wearing a fuschia-colored blouse that showed her full breasts to advantage, and her snug jeans made her waistline look just right. Jim's heartbeat had picked up when he first saw her, but now that she was standing next to him, he didn't feel as nervous. Her presence was familiar, and he liked it.

He ordered drinks, and after a little chit-chat he asked her to dance. He knew from before that when she was out on the town, her two boys, ages eight and ten or so, were with their dad, and she didn't have much holding her back. He could feel the interest building within him as he danced with her, his hand on the small of her back, her breasts pressed against him.

After the dance they went back to their drinks, and she said she had to say hello to a couple of people. Jim asked if she'd come back to dance a couple more, and she said, "Sure."

She was gone for over an hour, talking with this person and that, mostly men. Jim felt edgy now, his mouth dry. He didn't dance with anyone else because he didn't want to be unavailable, so he sat and drank. He put away three beers in the time he would usually drink two, and then at a little before midnight she came back to the place where he sat.

He put his hand on her waist, and she put her hand on his leg. He smiled and puckered his lips, and she gave a cat smile as she showed the tip of her tongue between her lips.

Then they were dancing, and back at the bar drinking, and dancing again, and drinking, and then finishing each dance with a long, wet kiss.

It was later now. The haze of cigarette smoke, the sound of the band, the thump of the dice cups — it all had the feel of late night. Jim knew he had been there for quite a while, knew that the curtain would be coming down before long.

At last call he hooked a finger into one of her belt loops in front and said, "You wouldn't make me drive all the way home alone tonight, would you?"

She smiled and hooked one of his belt loops as she said, "Of course not."

She drove first, and he followed. He parked on the street in front of her apartment house, and by the time he got to the door she had it unlocked and was standing inside, waiting.

Things happened just like before — standing beneath the light in her bedroom, undressing her and seeing the gorgeous breasts stand out. Then all of her clothes and all of his were on the floor, and the two of them lay entwined on her soft double bed.

He did not have to tell her he had been hungering for this, for he nearly devoured her as he ran his lips all over her body. He lavished his tenderness on her, loving her uptown and downtown. He could tell she was glad to be giving him the opportunity as well as enjoying the sensation for herself. She ran her fingers through his hair, then up and down his back, and then she clasped his buttocks as they worked toward the finale.

Grey light was in the room when he awoke. The air conditioner was running, and they had only a sheet to cover them.

Arlene of the dark hair was sleeping at his left. He folded back the sheet and saw one of the breasts that had held so much wonder for him, and he turned to it. She woke to his attention, and she responded by putting her hands around his head and holding him close to her. He felt as if he was floating, now curled and now shifting, his head buried in the silken pillow of her breasts. Then things became firm and fell in line; in a few minutes the two of them were joined face to face in the early morning light, and her legs were wrapped around him.

CHAPTER 4

The full moon was shining just like the night before. All day Saturday, Jim had thought about the rollin' and tumblin' at Arlene's place, and when evening came around he had the urge to go to town again. His hangover had worn off by early afternoon, but he was tired, so he slept about an hour when he came in from work. Then, by the time he got through with his shower, dinner, and dishes, it was nearly ten o'clock. As he recalled, Arlene had shown up at about ten-thirty the night before, so he thought he might be all right.

Back in the Trail's End, he saw many of the same people he had seen the night before. He bought a beer and ambled through the crowd, saying hello here and there, until he saw Arlene. She was sitting at a table with Tommy Moore.

Jim took another look to be sure, then went to stand by the bar where he would be out of their view. He needed a moment to absorb what he had just seen.

The last time he had seen Tommy Moore had been at the county fair, three weeks earlier, when Tommy had been escorting Jim's ex-wife, Elaine. Seeing him now was quite a switch.

Tommy Moore was the type of man Elaine would like to get a hold of. He had land and cattle and business dealings, and he drove nice vehicles. Like as not, he was in debt up to his ass like anyone else, but he cut a good figure. He always wore a clean white straw hat in the summer and a clean black felt hat in the winter. In addition to shined boots and pressed blue jeans, he wore long-sleeved western shirts, white or striped, with his monogram on the left pocket flap. He also had the monogram on the door of his white Ford pickup, as well as on the door of his white Lincoln Continental.

Jim remembered seeing the Continental shortly after he had moved to the ranch. He was hunkered down looking at the cattle guard at his front entrance when the white Continental stopped across the road, in the wide spot by Jim's mailbox. The tinted windows were rolled up, no doubt for climate control, and although Jim couldn't see the driver, he could see the TM on the door. Realizing that he probably hadn't been noticed where he knelt behind the fence brace, he stayed where he was. The car door opened and Tommy Moore stepped out, went to the front of the car, pushed down the hood and made a subdued latching sound, got back into the car, closed the door in the quiet way that new car doors close, and drove on.

Tommy Moore had looked clean and fresh and cool, and he had not looked around him at all. Jim remembered that impression. The man had seemed as if he carried his world with him, and even if there had been a moment's imperfection, he did not need to recognize any of the lesser middle ground he was passing through. When Jim saw him a few days later at the county fair, with Elaine at his side, the man showed no signs of recognizing Jim — even though they had known each other for years and had crossed paths at the livestock auction, in the farm and ranch supply places, and in any of a dozen other businesses around the county.

That was Tommy Moore, or at least Jim's impression of him. In his cattleman's way he was a man of fashion, a stylish bachelor in his mid-thirties, and some version of a playboy. If there was a book for people of his set, that book probably said it was all right to go out on dates with trim divorcees and to pick up sexy women in a country-western bar.

Jim drank another beer by himself and then took a stroll through the crowd. Tommy and Arlene were both gone, and the waitress was clearing the drink glasses from their table as two more couples sat down. Jim thought, it was probably also a part of Tommy's code not to stay a long time in the bar with a woman like Arlene if he could take things off to the side, quiet-like.

33

As Jim drank another beer, he couldn't help wondering how Tommy and Arlene ended up at the same table. Jim knew it was none of his business, but he wondered if Tommy had expected to meet Arlene or if he had just bumped into her. Jim also wondered if Arlene had it in for Elaine in some way. He recalled he had first gone to bed with Arlene when things had gone to hell in his marriage but he wasn't divorced yet. He had heard that some women were competitive and liked to low-crawl other women, as the saying went. That was possible, but regardless of how it came about, he didn't like the image of Tommy Moore taking off his hat in Arlene's living room.

He drank a couple of more beers and watched the crowd. He worked himself into enough of a gloom that he didn't feel like mingling or dancing. He told himself he had no right to feel jealous, that Arlene could and would go home with anyone she chose. Still, he couldn't get over the idea of Tommy Moore covering the women that he did.

Finally Jim gave it up for a bad deal and went out to his pickup. On his way out of town he decided to drive by the Westside, just to catch a look at Dusty. If the feeling was right, he might even go in and have a cup of coffee.

As he drove by, he saw her standing at the counter talking to the bus boy, so he pulled into the parking lot. What he saw next caused him to gear down and pull right back onto the highway. Halfway down the row of motel rooms sat a clean, white Ford pickup with a TM monogram on the door.

Sunday shaped up as a miserable day for Jim. He woke up early, edgy and unable to sleep, so he sat in the kitchen and drank coffee. At about nine in the morning, Jim heard music outside, so he went to the window and looked out. Brant was washing the dark Ford pickup with a rag and a bucket of water, and the pickup doors were open to let the music blare out. Jim poured more coffee and sat down in the living room

34

to look over a week-old newspaper. At ten the phone rang, which made him jump; it turned out to be a wrong number. Not long after that, Brant drove off, and Jim went out for a walk around the yard and buildings. All he could see was work that needed to be done, improvements that called for money. Here he was with a run-down ranch, a run-down pickup, a run-down house, and a run-down love life. It was the type of feeling that made a fellow want to get Sunday drunk, but one thing kept him at home. He had told Dusty he would call her in the afternoon.

One o'clock finally came around, and he dialed her number. As soon as she answered, he could tell something had come her way. She had probably heard some kind of a report from Tammy.

Jim asked if she might like to go for a drive, maybe go to the river.

Dusty said she didn't think so. She was tired from working the whole weekend, and she had housework to do.

"Should I call you back later in the week?"

"That would be all right," she answered. "You could do that."

When they had said their good-byes and hung up, Jim sat staring at the phone. Tammy must have said something, and for all he knew, Dusty could have seen who got out of the white pickup. He continued staring at the phone. Then he thought, if he was going to take the rap for chippying around, he was going to make the best of it. He looked up Arlene's number and dialed it.

No answer. He dialed it again, just to be sure, and he let it ring a dozen times. He imagined the phone ringing in the empty living room, in the empty bedroom.

It was past check-out time at a motel, and he doubted that Tommy had spent the whole night anyway. He was probably back out at the TeeEm, sacking up his laundry to take to the cleaners on Monday morning.

Jim finally got hold of Arlene at about five. She said she had her boys back and had to get them cleaned up and fed, and their clothes washed. After a little maneuvering, Jim had a date to meet her for a drink on Thursday evening.

Through the new week, Jim worked with Brant at fixing and replacing fence. He didn't enjoy Brant's company, and he found himself taking a dislike to the man's physical features, but he listened to the talk and put up with it. Brant was from Bakersfield, where the weather was hotter and the hay bales were heavier and the wimmen were hot to trot and the Mexicans all carried knives. Jim told himself that Brant would move on before long and take his stories with him, and that he could stand it until then. Meanwhile, Jim put in his time, fixed fence, and kept thinking about Thursday night.

As he drove to the bar he felt an empty feeling, a fear that he might be stood up. Once inside the Trail's End, he ordered a beer. He drank the first half of it in five minutes, fidgeting and wondering. Everything seemed normal in the bar, but Jim felt edgy. To occupy his mind, he tried to fix his attention on other things. He looked at the moose head that hung on the wall, and he recalled a funny incident that had happened in the Trail's End a couple of years earlier.

It had been on a week night like this, when there was no live music. The bartender, who was in his mid-twenties and went by the name of Pepper, had fished a customer into making a bet. The customer was an athletic young man in his early twenties who was staying overnight in town after delivering some gym equipment to the high school. The bartender hooked him into a bet that whoever could touch his toe to the tip of the moose's nose would collect ten dollars from the one who couldn't.

The customer, being a good three inches taller than the bartender, had an aura of confidence as he took the bet. He set down his beer and went straight over to the moose, looked up at its nose, and took a couple of steps back. He kicked high, shooting the leg straight out and up, higher than his own head but still a few inches short of the moose's nose. He kicked again and again, bringing his toe to about the same height each time, until he gave up and went back to his stool.

The bartender came out from behind the bar, sat on the end stool, raised his right pant leg up above his sock, and unbuckled a plastic leg from a few inches below his knee. He hopped on his left foot as he cradled the artificial leg in his right arm. Then he stopped in front of the moose head, reached up with the plastic leg, and tapped the toe of the shoe on the moose's dull, broad nose. The young man paid his ten dollars, drank up his beer, and left.

Jim remembered the incident and smiled, but he still could not push away his anxious feeling of the moment. He had waited all week, and now he was waiting some more, wondering if Arlene would show up, and hoping she would be in the right mood.

Then his worries went away when Arlene walked in at a little after nine. She looked cool and clean and freshly powdered, and her brown eyes were soft.

Instead of leaving her purse at the bar, she kept it on her shoulder and moved to a table with Jim. He realized they didn't have a great deal to talk about, and what he really wanted to know was whether her kids were at home. After a couple of drinks he found out they were, and with a baby-sitter. Then he worked the conversation around to mentioning the new place he had moved into, and he suggested she ought to come see it some time.

She said she would like to.

He said it had a nice view at night.

She said she bet it did.

Not long after that, they left the table for the waitress to clear off. Jim appreciated his pickup, the way it shifted and turned and accelerated and got them to the ranch in no time flat.

He had Arlene back to the baby-sitter by midnight, and as he drove back home he felt calmer than he had felt in nearly a week. There was a late-night preacher on the radio, covering half a dozen of the major ills of the world in fifteen minutes, and it all seemed like pleasant entertainment.

Back at his yard, Jim parked the pickup so he could look out over the valley. As he sat in the cab with the moonlight shining in he felt satisfied, pleased with having done what he had set out to do. He enjoyed the after-glow for several minutes and then went into the house. He was thirsty, so he paused at the kitchen sink for a long drink of water before shutting off the lights and going down the hall. When he turned on the bedroom light he noticed that the two wet spots had dried, and he smiled as he straightened out the sheet and bedspread. Then he undressed and crawled into the bed, which still carried a trace of her perfume. He slept well.

At lunchtime on Friday, Jim got a call from Ernie. The early deer season was going to start in a week, and Ernie had gotten permission to hunt on a ranch belonging to Brenda's uncle, up in Mendocino County. Jim was welcome to go along.

"Boy, that sounds great," Jim said. "I mean, really great. You can't beat that. I'll have to get a license."

"Right. And you might want to sight in your rifle."

"Uh-huh." A thought crossed Jim's mind. "Say, was this the camping trip that Brenda mentioned that night in the Blue Flame?"

"Oh, no. That was last weekend. We went just the two of us. While you were out slummin'."

Jim felt himself flinch. "What-all did you hear?"

Ernie laughed into the phone. "Nothin' much, really. I just heard you were out in the bars both nights."

"Well, I've done worse with myself," Jim said.

"I'm sure I have, too."

"Not to go into detail unnecessarily."

"Right." Ernie's voice chuckled.

"So anyway, back on the subject of this hunting trip. I imagine you'll want to leave a week from today."

"For sure. I'd like to leave at about this time of day. We'll have things ready the night before, and we'll both get off work at noon. And then we'll just roll on out."

"Okay. I'll be ready. What should I bring, other than my gun and my knife and a clean pair of socks?"

"A sleeping bag."

"Well, yeah. I guess I meant supplies."

"It's easier if we just shop for all the food. You can get the drinks."

"Like a case of beer and a twelve-pack of soda pop?"

"That's about right. And don't forget the square bottle."

Jim pictured a square bottle of whiskey with a black label. "You drink that when you're hunting?"

"We're talking about camp, Jim. Up in the mountains, away from all the riff-raff."

"Okay. I'll remember the square bottle. Anything else?"

"Ice. Split that stuff into two ice chests, and pack 'em both full of ice."

"Cubes?"

"Either way. Blocks or cubes."

"I've got it. Anything else?"

"You could invite someone else. Does that girl Dusty want to go? Brenda thought you might want to invite her."

"I haven't gotten any thicker with her."

"Oh, well, if you don't have anyone, we'll all ride in my pickup, and it's that much easier."

Jim tried to imagine Arlene painting her fingernails in a sweaty, dusty deer camp, and it didn't seem very likely. "That sounds fine," he said. "The three of us can ride in your pickup."

"Well, if we don't see you before, we'll see you then."

39

"Sure enough. And thanks for asking me along."

"Glad to. So is Brenda."

Jim hung up and finished his lunch, and after he had put things away he decided to call Dusty. He had said he would call at the end of the week — or later in the week, now that he thought of it. He dialed her number, and she answered.

After the preliminaries, Jim asked if she might like to go out sometime this weekend.

"Tammy and I are going to Sacramento to go shopping tomorrow," she said.

"Oh. I suppose you won't get back till late."

"Probably not."

Jim hesitated. "What would you think about tonight?"

"Oh," she said, "tomorrow's going to be a long day, so I think we'll probably pack it in early tonight."

Jim didn't want to get shut down for Sunday, too, so he said, "Well, I'll be gone next weekend. You remember Brenda and Ernie?"

"Sure."

"Well, they invited me to go hunting next weekend."

"Is it hunting season already?"

"The early deer season opens next Saturday, up in the mountains to the west."

"Oh."

"So if I was going to call you again, it would be after that weekend." Jim waited, and she didn't say anything. Then, almost blurting, he said, "Should I do that?"

"Sure. Call me when you get back. And have a nice trip."

"Well, it's not for another week, but thanks. And you have a nice shopping trip." For no accountable reason he imagined her riding in the TM Lincoln. "Whose car are you going in?"

"Tammy's. She's got air conditioning."

"That's good. Have a safe trip."

"You, too, Jim. Buckle up."

Jim felt the emptiness settling in on him again as he pushed the phone away from him. He had already decided he was going to stay home tonight, and now he felt as if it might be a lonesome time. Knowing that the Friday night crowd would be out didn't make it any easier. Then he decided it would be a good chance to clean his deer rifle, sharpen his knife, and get things ready for the next weekend. And if he behaved himself tonight, he might go out for a while on Saturday night.

When the next night rolled around, Jim felt the edginess coming on. He could imagine the music and the voices, people drifting in, women laughing. He would have to be awfully sick, tired, or broke to stay home tonight.

Once he was seated in the Trail's End, everything seemed normal. He had a beer in front of him, the crowd was milling, and the band was playing. It seemed as if no time had elapsed since the last time he had come in and sat down, or the time before that. He drank his beer slowly and took a good look around. He didn't expect to see Tammy or Dusty, and he had no surprise there. He did expect to see Arlene, and as the night wore on, he wondered if she would show up at all. *Maybe she has the kids this weekend,* he thought. When the band was on break he thought about making a phone call, but he talked himself out of it.

Finally at a little after midnight he decided to pull the pin and go home. He looked around at the happy crowd in the Trail's End, and, thinking they would get along all right without him, he walked out into the warm night. He fired up the pickup and started to head out of town, until the idea crossed his mind that he could drive by the Westside.

Driving through the parking lot, he saw that there was no TM vehicle at the motel. As he drove back out, he looked through the window of the restaurant. The place was empty except for a waitress sitting at the counter, and of course it wasn't Dusty.

41

Then on a hunch he decided to drive past the apartment house. He would at least see if Arlene's car was there. He wouldn't go knock on the door or anything like that; he would just look.

As he drove down her street he saw her car, the red Pontiac with the white vinyl top. Then when he was a few car lengths away from it, he recognized the pickup parked behind it. There was no mistaking the vehicle. It was an old, blue-black Ford pickup with a license plate rim from Bakersfield.

CHAPTER 5

They said it always rained once during peach season. When Jim woke up on Sunday morning, a drizzly rain was coming down. He went to the kitchen and looked out, only to see that Brant's pickup was not back.

He had not slept well, and for all the time he had slept and not slept, he had been plagued with one image. Three nights before, when he had brought Arlene to this bedroom, she had done something he had never felt before. On the second go-round that evening, she had reached under her own leg as she lay beneath him, and she had cradled his testicles in her hand, pulling him gently to her as she brought him to an explosive finish. Now he could not get that idea out of his mind.

At seven a.m. the sun was up but not visible, and Jim could see the world in grey light. He went to the back door and looked out at the yard that was soaking up the slow rain. Water dripped from the broad leaves of the fruitless mulberry tree onto the patio. Fifty yards away, almost in a direct line with the tree, he saw a wet rat in the lee of the woodpile.

He went for his rifle, the .22 magnum, and opening the door a crack, he took a shot at the rat. It did not move. He shot again, and the rat disappeared. He knew he had not hit it; if he had, the rat would have flopped over or bounced in the air. All he saw now was the wet, blank yard.

After he put the rifle away he fixed coffee and moped in the kitchen. He found himself harboring a strong resentment toward Brant, even though he knew Brant was doing no more and no less than he himself would do. It also bothered him to think that Arlene might put him and Brant on an equal footing, as if they were equally desirable. Disliking Brant as he did, even in the physical details, he found that idea hard to take.

More than those thoughts, he was haunted by the memory of her hand holding him. That impression mixed and blended with the other images he had of the soft, white parts of her body that yielded and responded. His thoughts ran full of breasts and legs and midriff, wet kisses, motion and clinch, sighs of approval.

By turns he hated Brant, then despised him, then merely wanted to top his work—trump him, cover Brant's work with his own. It didn't matter what Brant had done with her. He would do it his way, all over again, and then he would be all right. That was what he needed, to mingle with her body and feel the magic that came with being what he was for those few minutes.

He went to lie on the couch, but he couldn't stay still. The raw feeling ate at him, gave him the displaced feeling that he hadn't slept at all. Of course he had slept some, but he knew he hadn't slept off everything he had had to drink the night before, and this morning's coffee had jangled his nerves plenty. One good release would make a hell of a difference. He would be able to sleep then.

He thrashed on the couch a while longer, went out to make sure his pickup windows were rolled up, and then took a long, hot shower. At about ten, when he saw Brant's dark pickup come rolling through the yard, he took care not to look out the window and see the man himself. Then he went to sit by the telephone. He knew he had to do it just right. If he called too soon, she could likely give him the brush-off; if he waited too long, she would have her kids back and be caught up in her mom duties.

He made himself wait an hour, which would give her time to freshen up. He felt a stir as he thought of her in her house-coat, emanating the clean smell of a woman just out of the shower—clean and powdered but still damp around the ears.

She answered the phone on the second ring, and she seemed glad to hear from him.

"I'll tell you," he said, "I'm gettin' cabin fever, cooped up in this weather."

She laughed.

"I need to get out, and I was wondering if you might like to go for a drive."

"A drive?"

"Yeah, just out to the river and back, or something like that."

She didn't speak for several seconds, and then she said, "Well, I've got to pick up my kids at four."

"Oh, we'd be back by then, easy."

"Well, okay," she said. "How about if you give me half an hour?"

"That's fine. I'll be by at eleven-thirty."

Now he was a happy boy. He put on some clean clothes, looked himself over in the mirror, and went light-footed to the pickup. It would take him nearly twenty minutes to reach her place, so the dead time was over.

She looked nice as she came out of her apartment — fresh and firm. He helped her into the pickup and then hopped in on his side. At his suggestion they stopped for a six-pack of wine coolers, and then he drove to the river.

There were plenty of parking places along the river, and most of them were deserted today. He found a good spot in a clump of oaks, where hanging wild grape vines gave partial seclusion. The rain had slowed down to a mist, so Jim was able to roll down his window. Arlene opened her wing window and lit a cigarette. They sat for a couple of minutes without talking.

"I've really missed you," he said.

She looked at him and smiled. "Really?"

"Yeah, really. Sometimes it's all I can think about."

She blew smoke at the wind wing and then turned her brown eyes toward him again. "I thought I might see you Friday night, but I missed you. I thought maybe you had a date."

"Nah. I stayed home. I looked for you last night, but obviously I didn't meet up with you, either."

"Well, you got a hold of me today, and that's what counts."

He leaned towards her with his arm on the back of the bench seat, and she moved towards him. Then she leaned forward, opened the ash tray, and crushed the half-smoked cigarette. Their lips met, and he lost himself in the careless wet taste of wine cooler and cigarette smoke. Then he was kissing her chest, just below her throat and above her blouse. He could feel her steady herself against the seat with her left arm as she curled her right arm around his head.

In a few minutes he had her blouse open, her bra unhooked and slipped above her breasts, and all the clothes from below her waist neatly folded and stacked on the floor. She smiled as he twisted in the seat to get ready; then the scene closed in and they were in motion, constricted against the back of the pickup seat and the two doors, but getting the thing done nevertheless.

They dressed right away afterwards, then finished their second round of wine coolers. Arlene looked at her watch.

"Should we be heading back pretty soon?" he asked.

"Pretty soon."

They drank the last of the wine coolers on the way back to town. She smoked a cigarette and smiled his way now and then as he drove back to her place. He walked her to her door, tasted her smoky kiss, and left.

Rather than drive back to the ranch right away, he stopped at the Buckhorn. He felt satisfied for having done what he wanted so badly to do, but he didn't feel the radiance he had sensed on other occasions with her. Instead he felt empty, as he had felt at other times, some of them many years earlier, when he had done this thing just to be doing it. Those were the times when he left without staying the night, or had lain in his own bed with a woman who had turned into a stranger. Arlene wasn't quite like that, but when the thing was done, they really didn't have much to talk about. Except for leading up to the act, and then moving through it, they didn't do anything together. Still, he usually felt better than this afterwards, even if there wasn't much else to it.

Jim drank half a dozen beers in the Buckhorn, and by the time he left for home he just felt tired. As he thought of Arlene he felt a tired satisfaction; as he got closer to home and thought of Brant, he felt a tired ill will. The dark pickup was gone when Jim reached the top of the hill, and that much made him feel better. He parked his own pickup, shut it off and got out, walked quickly through the falling mist, and went into the house to be alone.

The next morning, Jim could remember a dream he had had the night before. He was back working in the peach orchard, where he had worked the year before he worked for the walnut and prune grower. In the dream, he had a trailer load of peaches jack-knifed against his tractor because he had tried to make too close of a turn between two rows. All of the pickers were pushing the trailer and jabbering in Spanish, as they had always done back then when a trailer got stuck in the mud. He wasn't in the mud this time, though. He was just stuck with his tractor perpendicular to the trailer, moving back and forth in little jerks.

Now in the light of day, he wondered why he didn't just pull the pin on the hitch, get free, and come at it from another angle.

That was the way it had been in the peach orchards, though — always tight. Coming back into the orchard he would park the empty trailer off to the side against one row, unhitch, back up, hook up the full trailer, and squeeze past the empty one as he pulled out. Only when he was at the end of the orchard, and out into the open air again, did he relax. Then he rolled along happy, looking back occasionally at the two tons of shining peaches that he was helping send out into the world.

He had always been glad not to have to stay in the orchard, where the air never stirred. It was all heat and humidity, peach fuzz and mosquitoes. Out in the open he would think of the pickers working their way through the orchard like ants, dumping their bags into a trailer that sat motionless with its tongue in the dirt until the boy on the tractor came back.

Always the part he liked best was pulling out of the orchard and feeling the fresh air on his face as he gave the tractor more throttle. He remembered that part now. It was better than the dream.

Over the course of the next four days, neither Brant nor Jim mentioned Arlene, of course. They spoke less than before, anyway, as Jim could not bring himself to be friendly. He initiated very little conversation, and he gave no more encouragement than an "Is that right?" to any of Brant's topics.

On Friday morning he let Brant go, paying him for a day's work on Friday but giving him the check and the dismissal at seven in the morning. Jim was getting close to caught up on the work, and he didn't have any money to burn. Furthermore, he just didn't want Brant on the place, alone or otherwise, while he was off in the mountains with Ernie and Brenda.

Brant took the news in stride. In one of his Bakersfield stories he had told of throwing his job in the boss's face and saying, "I was lookin' for a job when I found this one." As Brant nodded and looked at the check, Jim imagined that the same old outlook would hold the man in good stead this time.

Brant was gone by nine, and Jim was glad to see him go. Still, he admitted to himself that he had done a chickenshit thing by firing the man.

Jim met Ernie as planned at noontime. Ernie said the moon was down to a half-moon, so the deer wouldn't be feeding much at night. That would make the morning hunt better. Jim nodded as he handed his gun case to Ernie, who stowed it amidst the gear. As Ernie re-arranged things to accommodate the two chests full of ice and beverages, Jim became aware of an item he had seen but not registered consciously. It was a ten-gallon milk can, the type that had been used so commonly in the dairies of years gone by.

"Is that milk can full of water?" he asked.

"Yeah," Ernie answered. "I'm sure there's water in the place where we're goin' to camp, but I'm bringin' this along just to be sure."

Jim nodded and looked over the rest of the gear, which filled up the pickup bed. Then he helped Ernie tie a canvas tarp over the back, and they were on their way.

According to Ernie, it would take nearly three hours to get to the uncle's house, and then another two hours to reach the place where they were going to hunt. Brenda and Ernie were both in good spirits and they had a box full of taped music, so Jim worked his way into a good mood also as the pickup roared along.

They pulled into Uncle Calvin's yard at a little before four. The uncle came out of the house as Ernie got out of the pickup. The older man was probably in his early sixties, with a fringe of grey hair around a white bald head that looked as if it had never seen the sun. He was wearing a white undershirt, khaki pants, and dark suspenders, and he squinted in the afternoon sun. After talking a moment with Ernie he came to the driver's side and looked into the cab. He said hello to Brenda, was introduced to Jim, and then returned his attention to Ernie, who absorbed a long set of explanations on how to get to the ranch, how to get to the camp, and where the best hunting was. Then the uncle looked back inside the window and spoke to Brenda.

"I'm tellin' your husband here about that point where I've always killed deer. You know the place, Brenda. I bet I've killed nearly thirty deer there. Every time I've got one out of there, a new one comes and takes his place."

"Aren't you going to hunt this year, Uncle Cal?"

"I might, but I'll let you kids go out there first. I've got plenty of time, and I can go up there any day of the week." He

49

smiled. "I get plenty of enjoyment knowin' you kids are gonna go up there and have a good time." He turned back to Ernie and explained a little more about the layout, the gates, and the neighbors. Then he gave Ernie a key and let the young people get on their way.

They reached the camp in full daylight, but the shadows were starting to stretch. The ranch was well up in the Coast Range, so the sun went down quickly once it got near the mountain tops. The camp site lay in a grove of madrone and oaks, at the base of a cold-water spring. A cow camp and hunting camp, it had a rock-lined campfire pit, a wooden picnic table with built-on benches, a set of wooden shelves nailed up between two medium-sized oak trees, and a heavy wire stretched overhead across the table. It would do for hanging a lantern or a wet towel.

Ernie and Brenda worked well together, setting up their tent and laying out the kitchen gear. Jim rolled his bed out on the ground, with the assumption that he would take shelter in the pickup cab if they got any rain. With camp set up, Jim and Ernie went up the hill to a manzanita thicket and hauled back enough dead stuff for the evening's fire.

Dusk was coming on, and Brenda had three drinks poured and sitting on the table next to the square bottle. They toasted to a good camp and a good hunt, and then Jim started the campfire. It had been years since he had cooked on open coals like this, but the sight and smell of burning manzanita brought it all back. The dead brush, grey on the outside and salmon-colored on the inside, was iron-hard, hot-burning, austere wood that gave off little smoke and made a good bed of long-lasting coals.

Jim barbecued the steaks while Brenda laid out the salad, bread, and other items for supper. During this time, Ernie puttered around with his gear, going from the tent to the pickup and back. He brought out a gambrel, which was an iron utensil made of half-inch steel rod and shaped like an over-sized coat hanger with a hook on each tip. Jim knew what it was for — to hang an animal by its hind legs. Ernie folded up a paper towel, dipped a small gob out of the Crisco can, and gave the gambrel a rub-down.

Then he brought out a block and tackle — an old set of wooden pulleys connected by ancient-looking, tightly woven, yellowed rope. It had an iron hook on each half, so Ernie hung it on a low branch with the top hook and set the eye of the gambrel onto the lower hook.

"All ready," he said, with a nod and a wink. Then he went to the picnic table and poured another round of drinks, and a little while after that the three of them ate their meal at the table.

After they had eaten, Ernie poured water from the milk can and set the aluminum dishpan on the grate. He squirted in some dish soap, dropped in the dirty utensils, and then set out the camp chairs. By now, night had fallen, and the firepit gave off an orange glow. Ernie had a half-smile on his face, and Jim appreciated the seriousness with which his friend went about his tasks in camp.

"I'll tell you," Ernie began. "This is as good as it gets, isn't it?"

Jim could feel the warmth of the coals move up and down his face as he nodded.

Brenda said, "It sure is nice."

"Over two thousand acres to ourselves, and a padlock on the front gate. And to hell with everything down in the valley." Ernie waved his hand in the general direction.

"Well, now," said Brenda, "be nice. Jim might have been thinking about that nice girl Dusty."

"Well, the hell with all the rest of it, then. And we'll have a drink to her."

Jim lay in his sleeping bag, looking up at the stars. The half-moon didn't brighten up the night very much, but he could see the smoke drifting up from the campfire as it burned out. He thought about Dusty now, almost with hesitation. Brenda's comment had helped him realize he hadn't been thinking about Dusty very much — partly because he didn't want to think about the likelihood of that chance slipping away from him, and partly because he had been in the rut of thinking about Arlene and Brant and the hold that the whole mess had had on him. He imagined Brant was back in Bakersfield by now, or close to it; he had said that was where he was headed. The image of Arlene came to mind, purse strap over her shoulder as she walked into the Trail's End. Jim realized it was Friday night again. He imagined Arlene striking up a companionship for the evening, but the idea did not eat on him.

He thought again about Dusty. He really did hope he would get to see more of her. He couldn't blame her if she was peeved at him for hooking up with Arlene; but he knew she would know, by the general set of rules, that he hadn't done anything she could call wrong. No one had a gripe until the two of them had an understanding, and that would be a while yet, if at all.

Jim rolled over and thought about the hunting. This was a nice ranch — different from what he was used to, but pretty in its own way. The landscape was different, the brush and trees were different, and even the colors were different. It would be fun to hunt.

Then he thought of his own little ranch, unoccupied in his absence, waiting for him. At least he had something to go back to, something to start over with. He didn't have a single head of livestock, or so much as a cat or a dog, but he had a place. He thought of the gateway where the turnoff was, and he pictured the two little oak trees he had planted. He frowned as he lay in the sleeping bag. He hadn't thought to water the trees before he left. Yawning, he told himself not to forget to do that when he got back.

CHAPTER 6

Jim heard the alarm clock go off, followed by muttering in the tent. Then he heard Ernie come out, pump up the white gas stove, and get the coffee started. Jim could not see the moon from where he lay, and the early morning world was dark and chilly. It would take a little while for the coffee to start perking, so he could lie in bed a few minutes more. His tongue felt thick from the drinks of the night before, and he thought he could easily sleep another hour or two. But he also knew that chances like this were rare, and he wanted to make the most of this trip. He remembered the landscape they had driven through on the way to camp — dry grass, buckeyes, manzanita, scattered oaks — and he felt the excitement start. It was real deer country. They had seen a couple of doe-fawn pairs on the way in, and Uncle Cal had said there were several good bucks on the place.

Cold cereal, milk, and hot coffee made the hunters' breakfast. They sat in the glow of the lantern until they finished their coffee, and then they got ready to go on the hunt. When they had their gear in the pickup, Ernie turned off the lantern, and the morning went back to semi-darkness. Ernie started the pickup, and as the engine warmed up, the three of them reviewed their plan. Following the uncle's advice, Brenda would leave Ernie and Jim at the top of two ridges, then drive around to the bottom and wait for them as they hunted their way down. Brenda carried a rifle and a license also, so she would be hunting all along as well. Ernie put the pickup into gear, and the sky was just beginning to pink as they headed out of camp.

They drove out the way they had come in the evening before, then turned south before they came to the gate. Half a mile later, Ernie and Jim got out of the pickup at the same time, then split up. The sun was just clearing the hills in the east as Jim slung his rifle onto his shoulder and headed across the dry, grassy tableland at the head of the big drainage. He found the place where his ridge began, then stood a while to get the lay of the land below him. He could smell tar weed and dry grass in the cool morning air, and he felt his senses quicken as he studied the land. The ridge below him sloped down for about a quarter of a mile and then straightened out and formed a saddle, where he was supposed to sit for half an hour. He nodded, breathed in deep through his nostrils, and moved on.

As he walked down the slope, he unslung his rifle and thought again about how he would do things. The rifle he carried was a bolt-action .30-06 with a scope, much different from the .22 magnum. When he got to his point he would put a shell in the chamber, set the safety, and then watch the draw and the opposite ridge. If a deer showed up, he would put the scope on it; if he saw antlers, only then would he flick the safety and put his finger inside the trigger guard. He had had a nagging sense of guilt for not test-firing the rifle during the week, but with the other things on his mind he had not gotten around to it. He told himself that he would be all right if he could get the crosshairs on a deer.

When he reached his appointed place, he found a seat against a buckeye tree, where his shape would be absorbed by the tree trunk and by the brush in back of him. He put a shell in the chamber, set the safety, and began scanning the side of the other ridge. The ridge ran northeast-southwest, so the part he watched was in sunlight. He remembered that in the early season, the deer fed in the sun in the morning and in the shade in the afternoon. Ernie was giving him the best of the hunt on opening morning.

Farther up the canyon, the trees grew tall and bright green. Jim recognized the madrone trees, large and spreading, with mahogany-colored bark. The bushier trees, also large but denser, and a darker green, were mountain laurels, or bay. On the way into camp the evening before, Ernie had driven close to one, reached out the window and stripped off a few leaves, crushed them, and held them for Brenda and Jim to smell. He called the tree a mountain laurel, and Brenda said her uncle Cal and her father had always called them pepperwoods.

The trees looked stately and benevolent as they provided a canopy in the deep upper gash of the canyon. Directly below Jim, the foliage was lower and not so dense. Shorter trees, farther apart, grew in the bottom of the canyon, while thickets of buckbrush and manzanita grew in patches on the slopes. He let his eyes rove up and down the canyon as well as back and forth on the hillside across from him.

After about fifteen minutes of watching, he saw a deer inching its way out of the brush and low trees in the bottom of the draw. His heartbeat quickened as he saw the sunlight glint on what must be a set of antlers. Rehearsing once again that it had to be a forked horn or better, he brought up the rifle and found the deer in the scope.

Jim could feel his heart pounding as the deer came into view in the scope. It was easily a forked horn and might be a three-point, but the angle made it hard to tell. He took a deep breath and made himself wait for the buck to walk out into the clear. The animal walked slowly, nibbling and browsing, until it came to a manzanita bush. It was in full sun now, and Jim put the scope on the thick part of the body behind the front left shoulder. The center of the scope wavered above and below the deer, so Jim took another deep breath and readjusted his elbows on his knees. He found the deer in the scope again; now the buck was raking his antlers upward through the manzanita bush.

Jim knew that deer worked their antlers that way to rub off the velvet and to polish their tines. He had also heard it gave them some kind of gratification. He watched the deer drag his antlers up through the bush a few times, and then, confident that the animal wouldn't move for another second or two, he put the unsteady crosshairs on the front quarter and pulled the trigger.

The shot crashed through the morning air, first with a boom and then with a ripple as the sound floated down through the canyon. Jim looked at the buck with his naked eye and saw that it was still rubbing its antlers. He jacked in another shell and lined up his aim on the deer again. When he thought he had the crosshairs steady on the tan object, he touched off another shot.

This time the deer turned away from the bush and trotted downhill to the bottom of the draw, where it disappeared in the brush and the low trees.

Jim wondered if he had hit the deer. If he had — and he couldn't believe he had missed both times — the animal would go down into cover, stiffen up, and probably die. A hunter always wanted to follow up on his shot, but it wasn't a good idea to hurry.

Before long he saw Ernie appear on the other ridge. Jim pointed below, and Ernie nodded, then signaled for Jim to go on down. Jim nodded, checked his rifle, and began side-stepping down the shadowed side of the draw. When he got to the bottom he found a game trail with fresh tracks leading out toward the lower end of the canyon. The trail led through trees, mainly low oaks and buckeyes, that formed a grove but not a very dense one. He followed the tracks for a little ways and found no blood, then came up out of the bottom and went back to see if there was any blood by the manzanita bush.

Jim studied the dry grass, finding no blood but letting his eyes rove back and forth on the patch of ground at his feet. He glanced up and saw Ernie moving down the slope, and then he returned to studying the grass. The idea crept into him that he had missed completely and had botched up the chance he had been given. He looked up as the footsteps came closer. Just as Ernie raised his head in question, the sound of a rifle blast ripped its way up the canyon from farther below.

Ernie pursed his lips, then said, "Brenda."

Jim nodded.

They followed the game trail down the canyon in the direction towards Brenda, and as they walked, Jim told his story in a low voice. At the end he said, "I thought at first I had to have hit him, but I'm starting to think I didn't."

"I bet Brenda got him," Ernie said. "You say he wasn't moving fast?"

"Nah, just trotting."

"Just one shot is a good sign. I bet she got him."

When they came to the end of the draw where it and others opened out onto a large grassy bowl, they saw Brenda standing in front of the pickup. Her rifle was hung in the gun rack, and she was waving. She came towards them at a brisk walk.

"Did you get one?" Ernie called out.

"Yeah," she answered, with a broad smile.

"Where is he?" Ernie called back.

"Right by the pickup."

"Really?"

"Uh-huh. I drove up to him after I went over and made sure he was down." Brenda was wearing a tan cap, and now she was close enough for Jim to see the figure of a deer stitched on the front. He realized he had seen the cap earlier but hadn't really noticed the deer.

"Where'd you shoot from?" Ernie put his arm around her waist as she came up to him.

Brenda kissed him. "Across the hood of the pickup."

"No, I mean, where were you when you shot?"

"Oh, back over there, off the road."

"About a hundred yards."

"I guess."

Ernie patted her on the butt. "Good work. Let's go take care of him."

Jim was touched by the way Ernie and Brenda seemed to share their good luck, but at the same time he felt his spirits sinking. He could still picture the deer in his scope, tan in the morning sunlight. He had had a prime opportunity and had muffed it. When it came to the clutch, he didn't have it. He glanced at Ernie, who was taking out his knife and unfolding it. Well, it was done, he thought.

Jim helped hold the deer spread out as Ernie did the dirty work. The tip of the knife went in and out of sight; then the abdomen opened, and wine-dark blood welled out. Ernie was bloody halfway up his forearms, and he kept up a cheerful chatter as he worked.

By the time they had the deer field-dressed and loaded into the pickup, the sun had climbed halfway in the sky and was heating things up. Ernie said he thought they should get the deer to camp and hang it in the shade, so the three of them climbed into the pickup. Ernie was driving, and as the vehicle wound its way up the hillside to camp, he pointed out the window. "Down below," he said, "is supposed to be better hunting in the afternoon. That hunt we just took is supposed to be the best morning hunt."

Back at camp, after they got the deer hung up in the shade, they broke out some food. The atmosphere was jovial, but Jim couldn't suppress his disgust at his own shooting. "What a piss-poor shot," he said. "I don't have any business hunting if that's the best I can do."

"Don't be too rough on yourself," Ernie said. He was cutting open a package of apple strudel, using the same big clasp knife he had used on the deer.

"I just feel like a dummy. What if he hadn't run right out to Brenda? I'd have flubbed up the whole hunt."

"Nah," said Ernie. "Everything turned out just fine. And Brenda got a nice three-point buck."

"Well, that's true." Jim turned to Brenda. "I didn't mean to be peeing on your parade."

She smiled. "That's okay. You're not. I'm just sorry you're so down about it."

Jim shrugged. "I just don't feel like much of a hunter. You two invite me on this nice trip, and I screw things up."

"Hey," said Ernie. "You didn't screw anything up. You did a damn good job of barbecuing those steaks last night, you brought a mighty fine square bottle, and you didn't get drunk and piss on the tent." Ernie stuck his knife in the table. "You're a good man to have in camp. And you'll get another chance to shoot a deer." He lifted out a square of apple strudel. "Tell him, Brenda."

Brenda was still smiling beneath her tan cap. "I missed the first deer I ever shot at. We were on the road coming into camp here, and he couldn't have been fifty yards away. I was sixteen years old and nervous, and I missed him clean. Then I got real down about it, and my uncle Cal said, 'Don't worry. That's not the last deer you'll ever miss.' And he was right. I missed another one, later the same day." She laughed, and her blue eyes sparkled.

"Great," said Jim, laughing. "Let me at 'em."

Ernie unstuck his knife and folded it with a click. "I bet we could hunt around camp for a little while, and then try some of that lower country this afternoon."

Jim was feeling better. "Sounds good," he said.

Jim sat on a smooth rock, staring at the clear pool of water. He could see the reflection of the overhead sky. The canyon had gotten deeper and deeper as he followed it down, and he did not have much of an idea of what the country looked like up on top on either side. After walking down into the canyon for over an hour, he had decided he was on the far end of the afternoon hunt, so he had come back upstream a ways and found a shady place to sit. Little by little he became aware of the silent, motionless surroundings. At the upper end of the canyon he had seen a buzzard overhead, but since then he had not seen even that much life.

He would have liked the chance to take another shot at a deer, to make up for his bad work in the morning. It was evident now that he should have taken some practice shots before the season opened, and he realized he had probably had too much confidence after shooting the deer in the bean field. He had assumed the old touch had come back, but now that he thought more about it, he hadn't been able to hit a rat at fifty yards with the same rifle. Hitting the deer in the head must have been a lucky shot, a cause for false optimism. He hadn't deserved that shot. He looked at a dead tree leaning against the canyon wall, about a hundred yards away, and he wondered if he could hit it. Bringing his rifle up and around, he found the tree in his scope. He held as steady as he could, but the crosshairs still moved on and off his imagined target. He could envision the deer he had seen in the morning. Relaxing, he lowered the rifle and let out a breath. At least he knew he was a lousy shot. That was more than he knew yesterday.

He got up from his seat on the rock and followed his own footprints upstream in the dark, damp sand. The stream ran barely a trickle, an inch deep and a foot wide. He wished he had washed his face while he was at the pool, but he hadn't thought of it at the moment. Now he kept an eye out for another pool, and when he found one, he set his rifle and cap aside and knelt to rinse his face. The pool was about a foot deep, and the water was clear. The sand at the bottom looked like tan velvet, and for a moment he hesitated, unwilling to disrupt the beauty. Then he cupped his hands beneath the surface, splashed water on his face, and splashed again. He expected to look up, with his eyebrows dripping, and see a deer staring at him. But when he raised his head and looked around he was still alone, in a cleft of a shadowy canyon.

He looked straight up. The sky was a strip of hazy blue, and the canyon walls looked steep and difficult as they widened above him. Very little grew there, and he knew it would be almost impossible to scale either side. Even if he could, the glare and reflection of the sun would make for hot work. The best way up and out was the way he had come down in.

The long uphill walk and then the climb back to camp gave him a good tired feeling. Camp was empty when he got there. He helped himself to a beer and sat down in one of the camp chairs. Evening was coming on, and he had not heard any shots. The world was quiet enough that he could hear water trickling from the spring. Then he heard the pickup coming on a slow, uphill pull.

As Ernie and Brenda rolled into camp, it looked as if they had a set of antlers sticking up in back, but then Jim realized he was seeing manzanita brush that Ernie and Brenda had gathered for the evening's firewood.

Ernie and Jim had skinned the deer at mid-day, so none of them had much to do except drink beer, barbecue chicken, and watch the fire. They passed a pleasant evening, making small talk and projecting high hopes for the next day. At about nine o'clock, Brenda stood up and said, "Vell, Ole, I tink I go to bet now." She leaned and kissed Ernie and then left the campfire. After another hour, Ernie and Jim rattled their empties into the plastic bag and turned in, also.

The moon above made a pale half-circle in the night. As he lay in his sleeping bag, Jim felt calm and relaxed but not sleepy. The long walk on his own had done him some good —

the whole excursion had, for that matter, even though he had missed his deer. Tomorrow they would go back to the valley, and he did not dread it.

He imagined Brant was gone from town, but he couldn't help wonder if the man had stayed around for a last fling before he left. Jim thought of Brant taking off his straw hat in Arlene's living room, thought of Arlene's bare legs, and the idea did not kick him in the stomach. Earlier in the week, that thought would have churned him.

Jim looked at the moon and then rolled onto his side, where he could see again the smoke rising from the burned-out campfire. That whole business with Arlene had kept him on edge for quite a little while, and now it was after ten on a Saturday night, and he didn't care who might be with her.

Arlene was all right, he thought. She had never turned him down, which had always pleased him, and she did not cling to him afterwards or call him in between times. Jim imagined she was doing very much as he himself had done — and as he understood many divorced or separated people did. They went on a little bit of a spree, sometimes to spite the old relationship, sometimes to prove something to themselves, sometimes just to cover old work with new work and to make the best of the market while it lasted.

As generous as he felt in crediting her motives, he still wondered about why she played the field the way she did. If there was any element of association in her taking a twirl with Tommy Moore, there might be some buried motive in her going with Brant, also. Those things worked funny.

Jim shook his head. On the rational level, he could tell himself they were all just people getting laid, but deeper down, he knew there were connections. With the diseases a person heard about on the news, people talked about the idea that when you went to bed with someone, you went to bed with everyone that person had slept with. Aside from diseases, that was still an idea. He could not shake the notion that, whether she knew it or not, Arlene was making some connection when she went to bed, by turns, with Tommy and Jim. If there was anything to that, there might even be something to her dallying with Brant.

Jim frowned as he rolled onto his other side. He knew he had been happy as hell taking Arlene to the ranch and trumping Tommy, but now he could see he had Elaine twisted up in there somewhere. He did not know if Elaine had been to bed with Tommy, but the association was there, so at some level he might have been trying to out-do Tommy twice with one stroke. He felt a chill run through him, as if he had touched his hand against the slick wall of a dark, cold tunnel. When he was covering Brant, he was really covering Tommy as well, and when he hated Brant, it was as if he had transferred the hatred he would have for someone who was screwing his wife. Elaine would never have had anything to do with the likes of Brant, of course, but Jim realized that in his own mind there was a chain of contact from Brant to Arlene to Tommy to Elaine. He supposed that when he competed with either of the two men, he had both women mixed up in his motives.

Jim let out a long breath. Things were tangled up, all right, but he felt he was getting them sorted out. He had thought he had everything settled after the divorce, but now he could see he had stirred it all up again when he had seen Elaine at the fair. He had to get over the idea that Elaine might go to bed with someone else.

He could imagine Arlene with her legs in the air at this very minute, and he could smile it away. He hadn't been that stuck on her personally, anyway. Things might not be so simple in dealing with how he felt about Elaine, though. If he was going to move on to any kind of relationship himself, he had better be able to live and let live as well as live and get laid, as he had been doing.

Whew. That was a long groping thought, following the tunnel all the way back and bumping into Elaine. He had told himself he was done with her, and now he guessed he hadn't quite let go. He turned again and lay flat on his back.

There was really no lying to himself, alone in his sleeping bag beneath the pale moon. He had told himself he had wanted out of that life because it was so constricting, but he had known, deep down, that it was also because he did not want to stay committed to Elaine. He had quit. And then — call it denial or call it guilt — he had not let go, even though he went rolling in the hay to try to prove he had. Now that he admitted it all to himself, he could feel the weight receding.

In the morning, Jim and Ernie switched places as they hunted the two ridges again. They took it slow and came out at the pickup at mid-morning without having seen anything. Then they decided to hunt the steep uphill climb towards camp, where they arrived tired and sweaty at noon. Brenda said they looked like two happy bird dogs coming up out of a slough, and they all laughed. The three of them ate lunch, broke camp, and drove back down to the valley.

Jim felt himself fidget as he heard the phone make its sound on the other end of the line. Dusty answered on the second ring. "Hello?"

"Hello, Dusty. This is Jim."

"Back from hunting?"

"Uh-huh. Just got back."

"Did you . . . get anything?"

"Brenda shot a nice buck. I missed one. Probably the same one."

"Was it a good trip, then?"

"Oh, yeah. We had a good time. It was a great place, up and away from it all."

"Uh-huh."

"Gave me a chance to think — you know, sort things out."

"Uh-huh."

He paused. "And, I thought about you while I was up there."

"That's nice."

He thought her voice sounded non-committal, but he kept up his spirit. "Like I said, I got to think about things a little — think about what I want to be doing and what I don't want to be doing."

"Uh-huh."

"And I was wondering what you thought if I called you back later in the week, to see about maybe going out this next weekend."

"That would be all right, calling back."

"Good," he said, right away. Then after a pause he added, "Well, I guess I should let you go. And I've got some things to do, too."

"Oh. Do you have a lot of unpacking to do?"

"A little. And I need to get cleaned up. I soaked up a lot of dust and campfire smoke."

"Oh."

"So I'll call you later in the week."

"Take care, Jim, and thanks for calling."

The sun was going down behind the foothills as he walked out into the yard. He knew there was something else he needed to do, and then it came to him. He needed to water the two young oak trees at the front gate.

CHAPTER 7

Jim watered the twin oak trees the first thing on Monday, while the cool smells of early morning made the world seem like a gentle place. It was always like that on summer mornings, before the sun heated things up. Come afternoon, a fellow had to be careful touching the pickup body, and he had to remember not to leave a crowbar or a pair of fence pliers in the sunlight.

But now was a good time, fresh and peaceful. As he filled the fifty-five-gallon drum he had set in the back of the pickup, he could feel the cool metal sides as the water level rose. He had no idea how long he would have to haul water to the little trees — five years, maybe, or ten, until they were big enough to make it through the summer on their own. That was all right, he thought. He had decided to start something, and he would see it through. What he would need was some kind of a water wagon, but for the time being he didn't mind using the barrel.

He followed his usual method, which was to fill the barrel about two-thirds full as it stood upright in the back of the pickup, against the cab. Then he drove slowly down the hill to the front gate and stopped by the tree on his left. Using a length of garden hose, he siphoned off the first fifteen to eighteen gallons. Then he jockeyed the pickup around so that the tailgate was centered over the bowl of the other tree. By now the barrel was manageable, so he walked it to the back of the pickup, leaned it down, and poured the remaining water into the earthen bowl. He was watering at one-week intervals now, and he thought he might stretch it out to ten days by the end of the summer.

Back at the house, Jim set the barrel onto the ground by the water faucet in front of the barn. Then he went into the shop and rummaged around for his fence tools—posthole digger, shovel, digging bar, bucket of staples, fence pliers, small utility pliers, and hammer—and put them in the back of the pickup. After another moment's thought he put in a sledge hammer and a pick.

While he was in the shop he saw an empty matchbook on the floor. Brant must have tossed it there. *Dropped it at his ass,* Jim thought. He smiled, remembering the old man and the phrase he used to use when he talked about people who did things that way.

Well, he thought, it was well enough to be rid of Brant, even if there was still some work left that he had thought he might push off on the hired man. Work was work, and it was all his in the long run, anyway.

He had never minded working with a shovel or a hoe, except maybe in a sweaty peach orchard where the heavy branches grew down and the Johnson grass grew up, and barely a breath of air came through. That had been hot, humid work, and the sweat had poured out of him. He shook his head. That was someone else's work now, down in the valley. Things were more open here, and if the weather got too damn hot, he could get out of the sun.

For the rest of the morning he worked at a job that he hadn't been looking forward to but that he wanted to get out of the way. He had to tear apart and dig out an old corner brace on the far end of his permanent pasture. Any kind of digging in dry ground at this time of year was hard work, and he wanted to get the pick-and-shovel part of his job done before the sun climbed very high, so he went right after it. He dug down around the base of the three posts, then took the sledge hammer and battered the brace apart. By the time he had the cross braces knocked out, the posts were a little looser. With the digging bar he punched down further around the base of each post, loosening chips and flakes of hard, dry earth. Finally he pulled out the posts, which were half as thick below ground as they were above.

He was particular about getting the posts out in one piece because he wanted to sink some new, treated posts in the same place. He looked at the holes, which were dry and narrow. They reminded him of the holes where teeth had fallen out of the weathered jaw bone of a cow. He didn't like the idea of trying to widen those holes with the clamshell digger, and it occurred to him that ten gallons of water in each hole would make the work easier. So he loaded up the junk lumber, drove back to the barn for the barrel, and hauled some water. As he filled each hole, he saw that the muddy water did not sink in very fast. He imagined it would take the rest of the day for the water to percolate through the hardpan, so he loaded up his tools and decided to work on another part of the fence after lunch.

That was the way his work went for the next few days — one task or another, always quiet and difficult. He got splinters from the posts, scratches and stabs from the barbed wire. But the world was emptying out for him, and he liked that. He was rid of Brant, and he had decided to avoid Arlene. He didn't need the temptation or any of the complications of going for another fling. Sometimes he thought of how nice it might be to take a tumble, and then he reminded himself that he had a better plan to work on. It wouldn't hurt him to take time and think about things.

As Jim worked on his place, he recalled some of the impressions he had taken in while he was in the mountains. As he sorted through some of the images, he thought from time to time about the trees. Even the oak trees had been different, and others, like the madrone and the laurel, he simply had never seen down here in the valley. All of those mountain trees — from the largest pines and oaks down to the trashy little buckeyes — seemed to live by a different set of laws than the ones down here.

Here in the valley, even in the foothills where he now lived, there wasn't much wild land left. The acres were counted, and every parcel had its production or carrying capacity estimated. The foothill pastures were bigger than the flat, irrigated pastures down below, and some of the rolling country up above and beyond him did dip away out of sight, but it was all counted down. Some of it, including parts of Jim's place, would be thought of as poor country because of its productivity. It wouldn't raise much of a crop or carry many head of cows, but there was a way to put a figure on what it could do.

It would be an exaggeration to say that the trees were counted, but to some extent they were kept track of. Jim had noticed that if a large oak in a pasture or at the edge of a field were to fall over or even lose a big limb, someone would likely come around for the firewood. Except along the junkiest sloughs and the steepest banks of the levee, people kept an eye out for the firewood. Ever since the energy crisis of the early and middle '70's, firewood was worth the scrapping.

In the mountains, though, it seemed as if a tree still had a life of its own, out of the public eye. Down in a canyon or up on a mountainside, a laurel might live out its whole life without having a leaf crushed by the hand of man; or a madrone could grow to a great height, spreading and flourishing, and then die and fall to the earth without so much as a stick going up in smoke. Jim had been impressed by the amount of deadfall that lay so casually. It would have been the envy of many fellows he knew — men in flat-bed, one-ton trucks, hauling around chain saws and towing wood splitters.

Jim remembered having seen vast wastes of timber in the National Forests when he used to go there, but much of that waste had been the slash of timber crews. It looked like what it was — the by-product of what people called development. Even then, Jim had paused at the idea that someone could trash a whole mountainside, pull out just the biggest logs, and say he was developing the area.

At Uncle Calvin's ranch, which as yet had not been assaulted by bulldozers and Cats with hard-hatted men setting chokers, life seemed to go on on its own, behind a padlocked gate. Even to Jim's eyes, it had looked as if a lot of firewood was going to waste, until he made himself think deliberately that there was some good in letting nature take its own interrupted course.

Now as he thought about it, it seemed as if all four kinds of land were different — farm land in the valley, foothill land like his, mountain ranch country, and the vast, honey-combed stretches of the National Forests.

Farm land had it the worst. There was hardly a square foot of it that hadn't been ripped up and packed down by generations of heavy equipment. It had all been doused and fumigated a hundred times over with pesticides, herbicides, fungicides, and fertilizers. It was still the real earth, but it had all been land-planed, and now it was manicured by gang plows, disks, harrows, and ring rollers.

Even in Jim's life, things had changed. Most farmers he knew were dedicated to using machines and chemicals. Jim could remember when he was a boy, and it was normal work to hoe the corners and edges of a field to keep down the weeds, or to go out with a shovel and cut bull thistles in a pasture. Now, that was work for a spray rig or the Mexicans, if it got done at all. And around the houses and buildings, people sprayed what they once might have hoed.

Up here it was a little different. The ground was rough and irregular enough that a fellow couldn't get at every square foot with an implement. Productivity was low enough that a few oak trees had been left along the edges, years after their larger cousins in the valley had been dynamited.

The more Jim thought about it, the more he thought he'd like to keep from leasing out anything if he could help it. He had already formed that idea as a general plan, and now he mapped it out deliberately.

He would start with the bean field in back, which he would not lease out again. He would put it into permanent pasture, drive the lease-farmers down to the flat, and try to do without them altogether within a year. Then, as much as possible, he would try to get by without the big machines and tanks of chemicals. He knew his place would never have the rough, untouched wildness of a remote ranch, but he would try to let it live under its own laws as much as possible. He recalled the smell of the bay leaves; for him, the scent brought together the beauty and freedom of a country that had been left alone.

It was all a matter of how a person looked at things, he realized. If a man had lived all his life figuring tons per acre, or pounds of butterfat, he didn't see a rock or a tree as being worth much. Jim had known that view, had shared it, and had left it in the valley, as it now seemed. That was a good place for it.

Jim looked around him as he stood at the edge of his pasture. It really was a matter of how a person saw things. In comparison with Uncle Calvin, he was a farmer, even though he saw himself as being in between. Then out on the other end there were people lots worse than farmers. They were the builders of housing tracts and industrial parks, who never seemed to mind covering up good farm land with asphalt and concrete. A cherry orchard or an orange grove was worth a lot more per acre than a hayfield, but if someone had subdivision and urban development in mind, those trees themselves had little value. It was nothing to buzz down an orchard.

Lots of good farm land had gone under because it was in a good location for a better-paying purpose. Fewer people had actual contact with the raising of food any more, and many of them, especially those who lived in the city, didn't really know where food came from. They bought it in a package. The suburban idea of land use was based on the value of real estate.

When it came to land use, Jim was with the farmers. He had been happy when he was on their side — happy knowing he was helping produce peaches and prunes and walnuts and the other crops he worked in, down to the sugar beets. And all the time he had the dairy, he believed he was contributing to a good effort.

Now he felt the same. People ate beef, and he was going to produce it. He just wasn't a farmer any more. He didn't measure the value of land with their scale.

For his own part he had a sense of having moved into another phase of his life, a phase in which life was his own once again, and he could decide for himself how he wanted to do things. He needed to manage his life and his ranch as well as he could, but that didn't mean he had to strip every-thing down to its last two bits' worth of market value.

He smiled, realizing he had been tending this way for a while. That was why he had moved to the foothills, and that was why he had planted the twin oaks. He wanted to live and let the land live — he wanted to live off the land without sub-duing every square foot of it. Maybe he would get pinched out someday for not being financially aggressive enough, but he was going to try to get away with it.

On Wednesday evening, Ernie called to ask if Jim would like to go up to Uncle Calvin's place in another week and a half, to catch the third weekend of the season. Jim said he thought he'd like to.

"If you think of it," Ernie said, "you might sight in your rifle."

"Good idea. I haven't even thought about that rifle since I put it away on Sunday. I'll do that." Jim had a quick memory of the rat by the woodpile on that drizzly morning, and he thought he should sight in both his rifles while he was at it.

He decided to fire the rifles the next morning, when the sun would not be in his eyes. After making sure there weren't any field hands irrigating the bean field, he set up a target west of the house. He set one bale of straw on top of another, with a bulls-eye target on the top bale. Then he made a steady rest on the table on the back patio, and he sighted in the two rifles. The .22 was shooting low, and he adjusted it, but the .30-06 with the scope seemed to be shooting just right.

The smell of burnt gunpowder from the bigger gun reminded him of that morning on the canyon. It had been like magic, waiting for the deer to walk out of the trees, then seeing it appear, finding it in the scope, shooting at it, and watching it trot away as if nothing had happened. There was no sense wishing he could take those shots over, but it was good to know that the rifle wasn't at fault. If the opportunity came his way again, it would be up to him to bear down and make his best shot.

On Thursday evening he called Dusty. She had said he could call back and ask about a date for the weekend, so he got his nerve up and dialed her number.

As it turned out, she had to work evenings on both Friday and Saturday, but she said she could go to lunch with Jim on Sunday.

On Sunday afternoon, then, Jim picked her up at her place. She seemed distant at first — untouchable — until they were in the vehicle and moving. Then she said, in a tone of voice that opened a conversation, "I met a friend of yours."

Jim felt a quick, short jolt in the pit of his stomach. "Oh, yeah?" Then he smiled. "You already know all my friends."

She smiled back. "I was kidding, you know. But I did meet someone you know."

"Who's that?"

"Your hired man."

"Oh. When did you meet him?"

"Last weekend. Actually, he came into the restaurant twice — once by himself, and once with what's-her-name."

Jim glanced at Dusty and then back at the road.

"You know," she said, "that one you were seeing for a while."

He made himself say it. "Arlene."

"Yeah. She gets around, doesn't she?"

Jim felt like saying, "Not in as many places as she used to," but he decided to let it rest. Dusty had already cleared him by referring to the affair in the past tense. So he said, "Did he tell you he was still working for me?"

"No," she answered. "He said he had just finished doing some work for you."

"Yeah, I let him go. I was pretty well caught up anyway. But he sure got tiresome, with his line of talk."

Dusty laughed, and then in a credible voice she said, "Ah bleeve ah could drink one more cup of mud there, hon."

Jim laughed. "I thought maybe he had left town."

"He may have," she said. "I haven't seen him in the last week."

Dusty said she wasn't particular about where she ate lunch, as long as it wasn't the place where she worked. Jim drove out to the north end of town, on the old highway, to a new little hole-in-the-wall restaurant that specialized in submarine sandwiches. The building had once been a fruit stand, the type that sold almonds and olives and oranges and clover honey to the highway travelers, but almost all of those little businesses had been starved out by the freeway. Some of the buildings had been converted into homes; others had become business places for enterprises such as real estate offices, taverns, little restaurants, and an upholstery shop — none of which was guaranteed a long life span but all of which took their chances.

Jim and Dusty both had hot roast beef and cheese sandwiches on wheat bread. They talked a little about what they had been doing at work, but to Jim there seemed a hesitation to talk about anything important. After lunch he drove her home, and they parted in good spirit.

The next day, after Jim had watered the oak trees and was hoeing a few weeds around the entrance to his ranch, he thought about Dusty's remarks about Brant. She must have wanted to let Jim know that Arlene had been with Brant. Jim couldn't blame her for getting in a little dig about how Arlene got around; and the more he thought about it, the more he appreciated what seemed to be a friendly warning.

Jim looked across the road at the spot where Tommy Moore had stopped his car that day. He wondered what Tommy would think if he knew he was on some kind of equal standing with Brant.

Jim remembered the idea about going to bed with a woman and going to bed with all her partners. He laughed at the idea that Tommy Moore had, in some way, been to bed with Brant, or vice-versa. Beyond the humor, though, it seemed as if all that hootchie-koo wasn't as innocent as it used to be. Even a girl like Arlene, who seemed clean enough, could pick up something and then pass it on. And for that matter, she could just as easily pick it up from Tommy Moore as from Brant. Sometimes a guy liked to ignore good advice like the "No glove, no love" motto, but it wouldn't hurt to think about it. What people were saying nowadays was true. Things weren't the same as they were back before he'd gotten married.

As far as that went, things weren't so clean then, either. Jim remembered a time when he'd gone home from the bar with a real nice girl, and a week later the little fellow had a tear in his eye. The doctor brought out a tiny cotton swab on the end of a long thin wire, and he shoved it down the gullet of Jim's peter. There was nothing funny about that, especially at the moment. The stinging, searing pain had come back to him in memory a hundred times since then, and it came back now.

"It's not gonorrhea," the doctor had told him when he came back for the results. "But it's transmitted venereally."

Jim shivered as he remembered the old pain. That in itself should be enough to remind him to be careful. And if that didn't do it, he could try a more positive approach: Dusty had given him credit for not being on the relay team any more.

On Thursday, Jim met Dusty at the Blue Flame for a couple of drinks. She was wearing white shorts and a lilac-colored short-sleeved blouse, and her hair was tied back. Jim thought she looked more sun-tanned than she had at the beginning of the week, so he mentioned it.

"My mom's gone," she said, "so I've been doing all of her yard work for her."

"It's been hot, hasn't it?"

"Typical August," she said. "But you know it better than I do. You're out in it all day, every day."

They went on to talk about the work they'd been doing, and Jim explained that he was just about finished fixing all the fence on his upper pasture.

"You don't have anything on that pasture now, do you?"

"No," he said, "but I've been thinking about it."

"Oh?"

"I had a chance to get a horse a while back, and I turned it down. Now I'm thinkin' it wouldn't be a bad idea, after all."

Dusty's face was shining in the soft light of the candle that flickered in its open-topped globe. Her face had a look of interest as she asked, "Have you had horses before?"

"No," he said. "But I think I might give it a try."

"That sounds like an interesting thing to do. What made you change your mind?"

Jim shrugged. "I don't know. I guess I just figured that must have been what I was building the fence for."

That night, when Jim was back at his place by himself, he thought of his conversation with Dusty. It had all been pretty commonplace. Then he realized she hadn't made any remarks about Brant or Arlene. That was good. Maybe it meant Dusty could let something like that go.

Jim wondered about Brant, all the same. The man had come to mind as Jim had begun to think again about a horse. Now he wondered if Brant was gone or if he was still hanging out in the valley somewhere. Jim hadn't seen the dark pickup or its driver since that morning two weeks earlier. He hadn't seen Arlene in that time, either, and it was probably just as well. He could do without all of that, and now it was time to go back to the mountains and leave it all behind him anyway.

Ernie was breaking ice with his hatchet when Jim pulled up in his pickup. Ernie had said he would make the ice for this expedition by cutting the tops off of a dozen milk jugs and then freezing water in the plastic shells. Jim could see now that the decapitated jugs had expanded. As Jim stood by, Ernie explained that the ice wouldn't slip out because of the bulging sides, and so he had to break out all the ice.

With his left hand, Ernie held a frozen container upside down over an ice chest, and with his right hand he smacked the flat nose of the hatchet on the plastic bottom of the jug. Two chunks and a small shower of crystals and powder fell into the ice chest. He struck again, then tapped around the edges until the rest of the ice fell into the chest.

"It doesn't matter," he said, between blows, "if I ruin these plastic things. It was just an experiment." He tossed aside the empty container and laid down the hatchet. "These things were sloppy to work with anyway." He picked up another jug from the wheelbarrow, turned it upside down, and with both hands laid it in the bed of ice. "I think I have enough cushion by now," he said. Then he picked up the hatchet, rotated the leather handle in his hand, and brought the flat head down with a swift, fierce blow. The ice cracked and the plastic buckled. "Half-assed way to do it," he said, bringing the hatchet down again. "But we'll have ice." He looked up and smiled. "Be a bitch to run out of ice, wouldn't it?"

Jim smiled. "Oh, yeah. Damn near as bad as runnin' out of beer."

"Really," Ernie said, smacking two sides of the upside-down jug. "And speakin' of beer, we'll need a bigger supply this time." He slapped the jug with the broad side of the hatchet head. "Brenda's brother Claude is goin' along."

"Oh. Do you want me to go get some more beer?"

"Nah. Brenda got some. We're fine."

Jim thought. "Do we need to take my pickup, then?" he asked.

Ernie tossed aside the empty plastic container, then looked up and shook his head. "He wants to take his car, so I figured you could ride with him, if you don't mind."

"Fine with me."

"Then he can leave it at the gate, and we'll all ride into camp in the pickup."

"Whatever you folks have planned is just fine with me."

Ernie tipped over another jug and laid it in the ice chest. "Not that this was planned. He just called up last night and said he had some time off, so Brenda invited him."

"Oh."

"I guess he's not doin' too well. Goin' through a bad time, and wanted to get away from it all."

Jim's mind flickered with images of a cold blue deer rifle, sharp copper bullet points in brass casings, a flashing blade of stainless steel. He didn't like the idea of putting those together with a guy whose mind wasn't right. "Is he on some kind of junk?"

"Oh, no." Ernie looked up. "He doesn't use any of that shit, as far as I know. He's all strung out over some mess with another woman."

"I thought he was married."

"Well, he was. But in the last year, that all went to hell, and he got tangled up with some other couple."

"That doesn't sound good."

Ernie tapped his hatchet against the plastic. "I don't know the straight of it, but it doesn't sound good. Brenda's all worried about him, and she hopes this weekend'll do him some good."

Jim felt himself wince. "I hope so." He thought again of the gun metal, brass, and stainless steel. "I hope he's not too close to the edge."

Ernie lifted out the empty plastic. "Nah. Life just has him by the goo-nads for the time bein'."

Jim laughed. "It happens."

CHAPTER 8

Claude had a beige-colored Monte Carlo with air conditioning, so Jim had a smooth, comfortable ride on the way to camp. The two had known each other growing up, but Claude had been in Sacramento for nearly ten years, going to college and then getting a job, and Jim hadn't seen much of him. Now in the conversation he learned that Claude had been working for six years at an office job in an inter-agency motor pool — working for the state, going through all the bureaucratic rigmarole, but at least working. As Claude put it, a guy didn't kick a good job in the ass, not in these times.

His wife had worked for the state also, in the Department of Agriculture, as a secretary. "I was stuck away in a little corner," he said, "but she was right in the middle of the empire. Sex and back-stabbin' and gold-brickin' — that's all they know in those places. They spend all their time tryin' to get into someone else's pants or else tearin' down someone else's program." Claude had his arm straight out with his hand at the top of the steering wheel. He raised his eyebrows. "I guess it was just a matter of time till she met someone and got ideas."

"Uh-huh."

"He's some kind of an assistant program director — anyway, he's got an advanced degree and he's on the ladder, and he's split up with his wife, so he starts hittin' on mine."

"Uh-huh."

"And next thing I know, she and I are closin' down our joint accounts, cuttin' credit cards in half, divvyin' up the pots and pans."

"It wasn't one of those things you could talk about, uh?"

"Nah. She came home once at about four in the morning, with her hair wet. You know she'd been at a motel, or his place, or somewhere, and had just got out of the shower."

80

"Yeah."

"Of course, I was waitin' up, all worked up and over halfway through a bottle of whiskey."

Jim shuddered. He could remember some of that sensation. "That's a lousy feeling," he said.

"You're tellin' me. It's like someone kicked you with a pointy-toe boot, right up the crack of your ass."

"Really."

"Yeah, so there wasn't much to talk about after that." Claude looked at Jim through his sunglasses. "I guess you've been through somethin' like it. The big *D*, anyway."

Jim nodded and yawned. "Uh-huh, but I didn't have to deal with someone else hornin' in."

"You're lucky. It makes you have bad ideas." Claude turned down his mouth.

"I can imagine."

"But you get over 'em. Life goes on. Now he's got her knocked up, and his divorce isn't even final."

"You didn't have any kids?"

"No. Did you?"

Jim shook his head. "Nope. It could have been worse."

Claude adjusted his sunglasses. "It can always be worse."

It occurred to Jim that Claude had become, at least in his own mind, something of an expert on life. The last time Jim had really known him, Claude was a kid out of high school, needing someone a few years older, like Jim, to buy beer for him. Now he was an expert. That was what ten years and a sharp-toed kick would do. Jim thought that if he had had someone make a move on his own wife and take her away, he would have had more authority in the conversation. But he didn't, so he just said, "Yep."

When they pulled off the paved road, Jim opened two cans of Budweiser. He imagined Brenda and Ernie were doing the same in the pickup ahead of them.

Claude finished his first beer in about ten minutes and settled into his second one. "I'll tell you," he said. "It's a funny feelin', knowin' that someone else is screwin' your old lady, and you try not to believe it, but you know it's true."

Jim could feel his eyes squinting. "Yeah?"

"Yeah. I'll tell you, it's like havin' the brakes go bad on your car. You don't notice a change, day in and day out, and then one day maybe you drive another car or something, and you go back and drive your own, and you notice a big difference."

Jim was trying to follow the comparison. "So you mean, like, the brakes went out of your marriage?"

"Oh, no. I mean, all of a sudden I noticed things had gotten different." Claude took a drink. "I mean, she was actually better in bed. It had happened gradually, and I hadn't noticed, and then one night I did. I figured she'd learned something from him. I couldn't say what it was, but it was different. I knew I was in trouble then, and when she came home with wet hair — well, I knew it for sure then."

Jim took a big pull on his own beer. "Boy, that doesn't sound good."

Claude gave a tight smile. "It isn't. But it's all behind me now."

Claude left the Monte Carlo inside the gate as planned, and he and Jim crawled into the back of the pickup to ride into camp.

Ernie opened the sliding window in back of the pickup seat and spoke through it, his face partly blocked out by the rifles in the gun rack. "If we see one on the way in, Claude, you can get out on the off side, and we'll give you the gun."

Claude was still wearing his sunglasses, and the reflection of the afternoon sun flickered in them as he nodded. "Okay," he said.

The drive into camp proved uneventful. The campsite lay in long shadows, but it looked just as it had when they had left it two weeks earlier. The little stack of firewood looked the same, as did the firepit.

Brenda and Ernie set up their tent in the same spot as before, while Jim and Claude rolled out their beds on the ground. Then Jim and Ernie went for more firewood while Claude helped his sister set up camp.

By the time they settled into their camp chairs, Jim had gotten quite used to Claude, or to the new version of him. Claude seemed cheerful and relaxed, and a couple of times he said out loud, mainly in the direction of Brenda, that he was glad to be up and away from the rat race. Each time, Brenda smiled and said it was good for him.

Four steaks sizzled on the grill above the hot bed of red-orange coals. The smell of cooking meat rose with the thin, musty odor of manzanita smoke and mixed with the smell of dust and dry leaf. Fall was starting to come on sooner here than down in the valley, and the air cooled as the sun went behind the mountain. Ernie poured four drinks from the square bottle and declared that camp was officially opened.

"Now I want you to know," he said to Claude, "you don't have any hard act to follow. Jim missed a deer just big as hell, right where you'll be goin'."

Claude looked at Jim. "You shoot about like I do, it sounds like."

Jim smiled as he lowered his drink glass. "I hope you shoot better."

"Jim *is* a good man to have in camp, though," Ernie said. "You can tell by the way he manages those steaks."

"That's right," Brenda added. "That's what we decided last time, that Jim was a good man to have in camp."

"Downright meritorious conduct," Ernie piped up.

Claude looked at Jim, who said, "As I recall, that means I didn't get drunk and piss on the tent."

Everyone laughed, and Claude said, "I can see I've got something to measure up to, after all."

"That's true," Ernie conceded. "We've got standards in this camp. But there won't be any big pressure on you in the morning."

"That's all right," Claude answered. "I do my best work under pressure."

Jim recalled a remark he had once heard in response to the line Claude had just used. *You'll never know.* But he said nothing.

The beer supply consisted of both cans and bottles. Jim, who had bought cans because they were less trouble in camp, found out that Brenda had bought bottles because she knew Claude preferred them over cans. After dinner, Claude seemed to settle in for the evening. Something about the way he relaxed in his camp chair and held his bottle of beer reminded Jim of the way a man would set his cigarettes and money on the bar, let out a breath, and settle in for a siege.

Claude tossed his first empty beer bottle into the plastic garbage bag that lay open near the campfire. Ernie reached into the ice chest and pulled out another.

Claude accepted it with a smile. "Thank you, Mr. Denman."

Ernie winked as he brought his head down in a slow, exaggerated nod.

Claude twisted off the bottle cap, held it between thumb and forefinger as he raised his elbow, and then snapped the cap into the plastic bag. "I'll tell you," he said, "you can't beat it."

"This is all right," Ernie answered. "Your uncle Calvin is a real champ. It's hard to find a place in the National Forest where you can have it all to yourself."

Claude took a big swallow and nodded.

Jim pressed his thumb against the side of his beer can and said, "Yep. This is the kind of place where you can just relax and let your thoughts wander."

"Therapy," Claude said back.

Jim turned down the corners of his mouth and nodded, even though he didn't agree with the word choice for himself.

Jim felt his mind vacate as the four of them sat for a while without speaking, with the only sound an occasional tick or pop in the fire. Ernie picked up a long, narrow piece of manzanita and began poking at the fire, and Brenda yawned and then smiled at Ernie.

Jim felt himself break into a yawn. Then he spoke up. "Has he had any other hunters come up here since we were here?"

"I don't think so," Ernie said. He looked at Brenda, who shook her head.

"That's good." Jim looked at the fire.

After a little more small talk, Brenda got up and said good night to everyone. Not long after that, Ernie finished his beer and stood up. He folded his chair and Brenda's and leaned them against the picnic table, then set the ice chest next to Claude.

"That's a boy," Claude said.

"It's not my first night away from home," Ernie answered. Then he said good night and went to the tent.

Claude tipped up his bottle, emptied it, and flipped it into the open sack. The empty bottle clanked against the first one he had tossed there. "Another scalped Injun," he said. He looked at Jim. "Are you ready?"

Jim wiggled his can. "Just about."

With new beers they would be good for another half hour, Jim thought, and with Brenda away from the fire, he imagined Claude would talk some more. In a very little while, he did.

"I'll tell you," Claude said, "I really hated that sonofabitch that got next to my wife." He paused for just a second and then continued. "But at least I knew how to feel about the guy. I just hated him — still do, really — and it wasn't complicated."

"Uh-uh."

"You know exactly where you are." Claude looked at Jim. Jim looked back and nodded. "Uh-huh."

Claude took a drink on his beer and let the silence hang, as if he was still deciding whether to go any further. Then he said, "But there's this mess I'm in now, that I can't even find my own ass."

"Really."

"Yeah. A real mess." He cleared his throat and spit into the fire. "There's this guy I know at work. He and I are at about the same level, and he sort of buddied up with me. At about the same time, he seemed to be hitting it off with this chick that works with us — she's a couple of steps down from us, but she's a staff analyst, too, so we're all on the same general level. Anyway, he starts foolin' around with her, it looks like, and about the same time he's strikin' up a friendship with me."

"Is he married?"

"Sure. So I figure he's using me for a cover. If he and I go to lunch together, or have a drink after work, then he can use me as an alibi when we're not doin' those things. Anyway, that's what it looks like."

Jim wrinkled his nose. "Do you like the guy? I mean, do you get along?"

"Actually, yeah. Or at first we did. He can be pretty funny, and he's got some good stories. But deep down, I think he's a creep."

"How long have you been friends?"

"For quite a little while, really. Over a year."

Jim looked at Claude. "So this started before you were split up with your wife."

"Yeah. We even went over once and visited him and his wife at their apartment. I think the guy must have owed a lot of money, because they both had jobs but lived in a one-bedroom apartment. Anyway, we got rotten drunk, the four of us, on some Algerian wine that I imagine he got for about seventy-nine cents a bottle. They told us we should stay over, so LuAnn and I said fine, we'd sleep on the floor rather than drive home drunk." Claude paused.

Jim nodded.

"And in the morning I wake up, and I look to my left, and there's LuAnn under this quilt, and I look to my right, and there's this guy Randy, laying flat on his back next to me. I just looked at him, and he woke up, gave me this big stare, sat straight up, and didn't say a word. He got up and went to their bedroom. Still had his clothes on and everything. I tell you, that was rotten wine. LuAnn and I had a terrible hangover for the rest of the day, and he told me later that he'd been hung over all the way through the day after that."

"But nothing weird happened."

"No. Just that. And you know, when you get that drunk with someone, you're just glad nothing bad happened."

"I guess."

"So anyway, time goes on, and my wife dumps me, and Randy seems to be gettin' pretty thick with Margie. And there's no connection there, that I can see. Then one day after work we're having a few drinks, and he tells me he's gettin' it on with Margie. I really didn't want the gory details, especially since I was on the other end of one of those deals myself, but he goes on and lays out this tacky idea that he's doin' this so he'll appreciate his wife better, and she'll appreciate him."

"Rationalizing."

"Exactly." Claude gave a short, humorless laugh. "I mean, what do you say? You just go, 'Yeah, yeah.'"

Jim widened his eyes and nodded without speaking.

"Then the guy up and says, 'You like my wife?'"

"Jeez."

"I tried to downplay it. I said, yeah, I thought she was real nice. And he didn't say anything more about it."

"So, was he trying to get you into a foursome, or was he trying to pawn off his wife on you?"

Claude shook his head. "He was ape-shit over this Margie. He wanted to stick me with his wife. That's what it looked like."

"And what did his wife think?"

"Well, she's nice enough, only a little whipped out from the way he's been jerkin' her around. She just acted embarrassed whenever I bumped into her. Like, they had only one car, so sometimes she would come and get the keys or leave them off, and I would see her. Then he sets up these tweaky little deals where he asks me to deliver the car and she'll give me a ride back, or he asks me to leave off some papers for her to sign — you know, all these little reasons to put us together."

"And so it happened."

"You bet it did. He had moved out by then. I ended up at that little apartment on a Friday night, and one thing led to another, and you'd think she'd been starvin' for sex."

"Really."

"Oh, yeah. We went at it. Then I heard all the stories, how he told her she wasn't any good in bed, that she didn't excite him any more, and all that. Meanwhile he's been bangin' his brains out with Margie."

"Of course."

Claude took a swallow of beer. "And I'll tell you, there's nothing wrong with her, not in bed, except she doesn't want to let me go home. Other than that, she's sweet as a peach, and he's just puttin' her through all that shit so he can play his mind game."

"Sure."

"And me, I say, hell, take what you can get. At that point I said, there's no rules. Someone did this to me, and now it's my turn. She's right in there with a smile and a good word, and he doesn't even care, 'cause he's off dippin' Margie. So I say, hell, go for it."

Jim widened his eyes again and took a breath. "I guess so."

"But naturally, things didn't stay that way."

Jim nodded.

"Next thing I know, he's tellin' her what a slut she is for screwin' his friend, but he doesn't say a thing to me about it."

"Like at work?"

"Exactly. I see him day in and day out, and he acts like nothing ever happened."

"So he sets you up with his wife, harasses her about it, and doesn't say anything to you?"

"Right. And if you ask me, that's just a little bit twisted."

"I can see why you might think he's a creep."

Claude widened his eyebrows. "Oh, hey, the creep part is extra."

Jim took a drink of beer. "Really?"

"Yeah. You'll appreciate this. You've got kind of an idea of what the guy's like already."

Jim shrugged. "Sort of."

"Well, a few years back, when they hadn't been married very long, they lived in a two-bedroom duplex, and her sister came to live with 'em for a while. Well, Randy drills a little peep hole from their bedroom closet, so he can spy on the sister when she's in the bathroom."

"How'd he get caught?"

"He told the sister about it. He tried to put the make on her, and when she tried to get him to cool it, he told her he'd already seen her naked, so they were halfway there already." Claude took a drink and gave Jim a matter-of-fact look. "The sister didn't go for it."

"I guess not." Jim's thought flickered. "I don't suppose you heard this from him."

"Oh, no. I got it from her."

"The wife. Not the sister."

"Right. After I'd been gettin' to know her a little better, you might say, I got to hearin' some of these stories. Most of 'em are about what a shit-heel he is, but I think this one tops 'em all."

"So, are you still seein' her?"

"No, I've been tryin' to break it off. Somewhere in there, I have this creepy feeling that he's in the middle of it. I mean, it's not just good ol' bangin' for the fun of it, her and me. It's like I'm screwin' him, too. So I'm tryin' to ease out."

"Probably not a bad idea."

"In a world of bad ideas, it's one of the better ones."

"What's the wife's name, anyway?"

Claude looked at his beer bottle and then said, "Elaine."

"That was my wife's name, too."

"Yeah. I knew that." Claude took a drink of his beer. "Entirely different person, of course."

CHAPTER 9

Saturday morning came early, with the sound of Ernie pumping up the stove to make coffee. Jim huddled in his sleeping bag until he heard the coffee pot start to plunk, and then he got up. Ernie was sitting in the lantern light, poking at the dead ashes with a stick, when Jim sat down and began to lace his boots.

"It's gonna be a good day," Ernie said.

"I hope so."

Claude came into the lantern light, and as Jim looked up to say good morning, he saw that Claude was wearing a pistol. Jim had understood that Claude was going to hunt with Brenda's rifle, the .243, so he was surprised to see the pistol. He had imagined Claude as being unarmed, or not having brought a gun, and now the picture was different. It wasn't strange to see a pistol, though — plenty of California hunters carried one, especially in the early season when the weather was still warm. The possibility of seeing a snake gave enough reason for someone to carry a sidearm. Probably not very many snakes died as a result, but a lot of hunters were no doubt pleased at the idea of being prepared. Now that Jim saw Claude in that pose, the image fit well enough.

Ernie set out four coffee cups and poured them full. As he set out cereal and milk, Brenda came into the light and sat down. After an exchange of good-mornings she bent to lace up her boots, and the strain on her face made her resemble her brother even more than usual. She was wearing her tan cap with the deer design on it, and Claude was wearing a similar cap, except that it advertised Scooter's Bar and Grill. He had been bare-headed the evening before, and his hair was shorter and wavier than Brenda's, but now the difference was less noticeable. Jim also noticed they had the same blue eyes.

Brenda looked up, and her face relaxed into a smile. "You gonna shoot one today, Jim?"

"I'll give it a try if I get a chance."

She looked at Claude. "How 'bout you, Boo-boo?"

Claude smiled, but it was not an easy smile like Brenda's. "Whatever happens," he said.

Ernie hunted the same ridge he had hunted on opening morning, Claude hunted the ridge that was now known as "the ridge where Jim missed the big one," and Jim hunted the next ridge to the south. Given the layout of the land, Ernie and Claude would be hunting together, and Jim would be more or less on his own.

The sun came up warm and brilliant as Jim wandered down his ridge, keeping a steady gaze on the pale, dry, grassy slopes where an occasional scrub oak cast a dark shadow. The canyon that lay between Claude and Ernie was deeper and greener than this draw. Jim appreciated the broad, open landscape as he loafed along. With just oaks and grass, and here and there a clump of manzanita, the country seemed uncomplicated, and that was what he wanted. He was glad not to be on the same canyon as Claude.

Jim hunted at a slow pace, taking a few quiet steps and then stopping for a while, trying to merge with his surroundings. When it was convenient, he stood or crouched in front of an object — a tree, a bush, a rock — that might absorb his shape. Each time he stopped, it took a few minutes until it seemed as if the normal sounds or rhythms resumed. When they did, he felt as if he was doing things right, as if the world for that moment was the way it should be.

In spite of his discipline, Jim imagined he would see few deer unless Claude kicked one out his way, and as it turned out, he was right. When he got to the bottom he had not seen a deer.

Nor had he heard a shot. When he reached the spot where Brenda was to wait with the pickup, Jim saw Brenda and Claude standing by the front of the pickup, drinking coffee. The rifle was in the gun rack, and Jim had the sense that Brenda and Claude had been in a serious conversation and were closing it up for the time being. Jim didn't think he was disturbing anything at this point, so he walked up and joined them, leaving his rifle slung on his shoulder. Brenda offered him a cup of coffee, and he said he didn't care for one. The three of them waited another ten minutes, and then Ernie came out of the canyon and into view.

Jim and Claude climbed into the back of the pickup while Ernie and Brenda crawled into the cab. Ernie said it would be a good idea to look over some parts of the ranch they hadn't seen before, so he drove back up on top to a tableland south of the place where they had been hunting. Jim and Claude stood in back, leaning on the cab and watching.

The mesa was mostly grass, and the hunters could see at a glance that there weren't any deer. As the pickup rumbled along, a jackrabbit bolted up in front of the driver's side and ran straight ahead along the dirt road. It stopped at about seventy yards out and sat straight up with its ears erect.

Ernie stopped the pickup. "You want to take a practice shot with the .243, Claude?"

Claude spoke through the sliding window into the cab. "I'd like to dust him with my .38," he said.

"Okay," Ernie answered back. "Have at it." He shut off the engine.

Claude unsnapped the leather strap that ran behind the hammer of the .38, then pulled out the pistol and raised it over the cab. It was a deadly-looking weapon with a dull, blue-black sheen. It had a four-inch barrel protruding from a thick body, and the bulging cylinder moved as Claude drew back the hammer with a click. Bending at the knees, he held the pistol with both hands as he steadied it on the roof of the pickup cab.

The shot made a brutal blast in the still morning air, and the bullet kicked up dust on the road beyond the jackrabbit, which did not move.

"Shootin' high," Ernie called out.

The hammer clicked and the cylinder moved, and then a second shot ripped the air. Again the shot went high, but this time the jackrabbit shook its head, as if the vibration of the passing bullet had tickled its ears. All four people broke out laughing, and before Claude could get set for another shot, the rabbit broke into a zig-zag run and disappeared over the rise ahead.

Ernie fired up the engine, said something to Brenda that Jim couldn't catch, and put the pickup into gear. The vehicle rumbled on for another two hundred yards or so, and then the road dipped down.

Ernie spoke through the slider. "I think we're coming up to a parcel that Calvin sold off," he said. "We can just cross it and get back onto his place."

Jim looked over the cab and saw where the road came to a gate, about a quarter mile ahead. When they came to that point, Ernie stopped the pickup and Claude jumped down to open the gate. He unhooked the gate, which was just a post with four strands of barbed wire, and dragged it aside to let Ernie drive through. He closed the gate, poking the post into a loop of wire at the bottom and then slipping an upper loop over the top of the post. Jim had turned to watch him and was taken by surprise when he heard a strange voice.

"Don't come any farther."

Jim turned and saw a woman coming their way, walking out of a grove of scrub oaks. She was a young woman, probably not much over twenty, wearing nothing more than a grey tank top and a pair of light-blue underpants. She had a muddy sun tan and stringy light brown hair, but her shape was pleasing to the eye.

She raised her right hand and waved it, saying again, "Don't come any farther."

"Is this private property?" Ernie called out.

"This is all private property," she said, coming closer.

Claude walked forward and stood by Ernie's door. "We're hunting on Cal Rainbolt's property," he said. "I'm his nephew. Claude Rainbolt."

A voice came from behind the young woman. "You're not on his property any more."

Jim looked beyond the woman and saw a tall, thin man headed their way. He had wispy red hair and a beard, a pair of rimless glasses, a bare upper body, and a pair of white trousers. Like his companion, he was barefoot. He looked to be in his mid- to late twenties.

"Who are you?" he asked.

Claude jerked his chin toward the woman. "I just told her. I'm —"

"Who *are* you?"

"If you'd shut up and listen, I'll tell you. I'm Claude Rainbolt, and we're hunting on my uncle's place, and —"

"You're hunters. That's what you are."

Jim could hear impatience as Claude said, "Yeah."

"Well, I don't like hunters. And I don't like people shooting on my property." The man's voice was quavering, but Jim thought he showed pretty good nerve as he said, "I don't approve of people discharging firearms on my property, and I wish they would respect my signs."

"What signs?" Claude answered.

"Up on that ridge, where my land begins." The skinny man pointed with his right hand, which had a gauze bandage wrapped across the palm. Jim saw a line of oak trees they had passed through.

Ernie spoke up. "Then your land doesn't begin right here, where the gate is."

"No, this fence was here before. It's not a boundary."

"Well, it's our mistake, then," Ernie said. "We're sorry."

At that point a third person joined the other two and pushed in front of the first woman. The newcomer was naked all the way, with long dark hair and a dark bush, a slender body, a gaunt face, and glazed blue eyes. "Get out!" she shouted. "Get the fuck out!"

Jim let his glance rove over her. She was probably the oldest of the three. She seemed unreal, maybe because of her detached look and her lack of modesty, but she was definitely there in the flesh. As Jim continued to gaze, he noticed a thin chain necklace hanging around her waist, with a small medallion dangling beneath her navel. She was just a hippie, that was all — maybe a little out of her tree, and not very stimulating because of her hostile tone.

The first woman's voice came from behind. "We hate hunters!"

Then the naked one, still with a glazed look in her eyes, began chanting, "Fucking hunt-ers! Fucking hunt-ers!" The younger woman joined in, adding her voice to the chant.

All through the encounter, Jim had had a sense of the presence of Claude's pistol. Ernie no doubt did, too, and Claude might have made some movement that Jim didn't catch, because Ernie told him to get back into the pickup. When Claude crawled into the box, the women quit chanting.

Ernie began to make his apology again to the red-haired man, who said, "I just wish you would leave."

Ernie said, "Well, if you open the gate, I'll just back right out. I'm sorry."

The thin man nodded and went to the gate. He pressed against the post with his bandaged hand, slipped off the loop, and dragged the gate open. As Ernie backed up the pickup, the man gave a

96

look of disdain and said, "You people ought to learn some manners." Then the pickup was through the gate, and turned around, and back on the road to Uncle Cal's property.

No one said much as Ernie drove back to camp. After a slow, bouncing, winding trip, Jim was glad to see the camp came into view. The pickup stopped at the edge of the camp site, and Jim felt a little stiff as he jumped down.

As the hunters sat around waiting for lunchtime, Claude became animated about the encounter they had had. "Can you believe that shit? Learn some manners!"

"Well," Ernie said, "they thought we were shooting on their property. We really hadn't, but they didn't know." Ernie paused for a second, then said, "And we did trespass. There *was* a sign on that oak tree, even if we didn't see it on the way in."

"Hippie-dippies," Claude called out. "Groovy people." He took off his cap and put it back on. "I bet Uncle Calvin wishes he hadn't sold that parcel — that one, or the others over on that end of the place."

"He probably thought it was a good idea at the time," Ernie said. "Some of those cabin sites brought him a good little sum of money, and it probably helped him keep this place."

"It could be worse," Jim said. "He could have sold some logging rights."

"Yeah," Claude said. "Those sons of bitches would shoot all the deer. Those loggers are as bad a poachers as you'll find."

"I bet our new friends don't each much venison at all," Ernie said with a smile.

"Naw, they're too groovy." Claude rubbed his nose with his thumb.

"Aw, shit," Jim said. "They just want to get away from all the assholes just like the rest of us do. You can't blame 'em for that."

"Yeah, but 'learn some manners'? The way they talk, and the way they run around with no clothes on?"

Jim laughed. "The one in panties wasn't too bad, but the other one was something else. For as decent a shape as she had, I don't think I've ever seen a less interesting naked woman."

"Really." Claude said. "I bet she screws like a mink, though." He reached into the ice chest and brought out a beer. "Do you think that keeps him skinny, tryin' to take care of both of them?"

Brenda's voice put a pang of embarrassment through Jim. "My God, you guys. The way you talk about women."

Claude was the only one having a beer. As a general rule, the rest of them didn't drink if they were going to go back out and hunt. Claude seemed to realize it as he asked around and everyone else declined. As he twisted off the cap he said, "I think I'll have just this one."

After lunch, Claude unfolded a map he had found in Ernie's glovebox. He spread it out on the picnic table, and Jim saw that it was a National Forest map, with mostly green shaded areas.

"I love the names they have for some of these places," Claude said. "Buck Point. Doe Peak. Deer Mountain. I bet there's not a deer on any one of 'em." After a little while he said, "Now there's a place. Buzzard's Roost. That's where we should go. How far is it, Ernie?"

Ernie looked at the spot where Claude's finger was pointing, and his pronunciation sounded as if he was correcting Claude's. "Buzzard Roost? That looks like damn near a whole day on slow roads."

"But by God, don't you think we ought to go there, to see what kind of a place has got a name like Buzzard's Roost?"

With his current line, Claude reminded Jim of the type of person who liked to move the party to somewhere else. Then it would be his party.

Ernie shrugged. "I guess we could go there some time, but it would have to be on a separate trip. And I don't know why we'd want to go to the National Forest at a time like this, when we have private property to hunt on."

"Well, I think we should go some time. All of us."

"Sure," Ernie said. "We can do that."

Claude looked at Jim, who nodded. But inside, Jim knew they would probably not ever go to Buzzard Roost together.

That afternoon they hunted below the camp, down the canyons where Jim had gone by himself two weeks earlier. It was a hot, sweaty hunt, and there was a general tone of weariness when they met back at the pickup. There was still plenty of daylight left, but they agreed they had hunted enough for the day. They got into the pickup and headed back to camp.

As they were winding their way back up the grade, they came to a place where the road leveled off and went straight in the shade of the mountainside. Across a little gully on the right was a string of buckeye trees, about forty yards away.

"Look at that," Claude spoke out. He slapped on the roof of the cab.

Ernie stopped the pickup and spoke quietly through the slider. "See something?"

"Hornet's nest. Hangin' down from that tree."

Jim looked where Claude was pointing, and he saw a grey-brown hornet nest hanging down from a branch. It was nearly as big as a person's head, but wide at the top and narrowing down.

"Let me see if I can hit it," Claude said.

Ernie pushed the gearshift into neutral. "You gonna use your .38 again?"

"Yeah. Just for fun." Claude unsnapped his pistol and pulled it out, clicked the hammer to move a shell into position, and sighted the pistol with both hands.

Jim watched the pistol jump as the gunfire shattered the still mountain air. He looked at the paper nest and saw a dark dot near the top.

"Hit it," said Claude.

"Is that enough?" Ernie asked. "Or do you want to shoot it again?"

"Nah, that's good enough," Claude answered, settling the handgun back into its holster.

Back at camp, Claude reminded the rest of the group of what a pretty black hole he had put in his target.

Ernie said, "I don't like to mess with those hornets' nests. I almost put my hand on one, the last time we were up here. I was pulling my way up a steep little washout, and there it was, stuck to the underside of a rock I almost grabbed."

"I'll tell you," Claude went on, "it'd be interesting to blow up that one down there with a shotgun, but I wouldn't want to get that close."

"I used to get 'em in the orchards," Jim said. "You'll be knockin' prunes or almonds with a pole, and you'll hit one of their nests and not see it. They'll follow that pole right down to the source, and zap! They get you in the face."

Claude stretched his elbows out and flexed his arms. "They'd have a hell of a time tracing a pistol shot." Then he patted the handle of his gun. "Nice thing about this little helper. It barks here and bites over there."

CHAPTER 10

Jim lay in his sleeping bag and looked at the moonlit sky. He had done plenty of walking in the morning and afternoon hunts, and he had put down half a dozen beers in addition to a couple of splashes from the square bottle, but he wasn't sleepy. No sounds came from any of the others, and Jim imagined they were all asleep.

The whole excursion had begun to eat on him, even though Claude had not told any new stories about his troubles in Sacramento. Despite Claude's comments about what good therapy it was to be away from it all, he brought enough of it with him that the therapy was questionable. He seemed to be wound up as tight as a Big Ben double-bell alarm clock, and Jim could feel the tension. He could feel Brenda's worry and Ernie's quickness to smooth things over, and even Ernie's patience seemed to be wearing. Jim had always liked Claude, but he didn't have much feeling for him now, and he didn't share Brenda's worry. He hadn't minded listening to the stories, as they had been peculiar and interesting in their tawdry detail, but he couldn't imagine anything he could do to help — except listen. So if he did that and kept it all at a distance, he supposed none of it would rub off.

Jim had thought of Dusty when he had been hunting by himself in the morning and afternoon, and now he thought of her again. Things had been going well with her since he had been up here last time and had been able to think things through. She seemed to understand that he had been through his own dreary phase and that he was trying to make sure he had come out on the other side of it. They had parted on good terms, with the agreement that he would call when he got back.

They were both being careful — both avoiding major issues, both avoiding mention of what they felt or would like to see happen. That was not the worst way to be, he thought. It was easy to get into a relationship too fast and then have to get out. For all he knew he might be out of this one before he got into it very far, but that would be all right, too. At least it wouldn't be messy.

It was hard to tell what would make a good relationship — that is, a lasting one. Ernie had once told Jim that he and Brenda had gone through a rough time, had talked about separating, but had made it through. Ernie had grown up poor in a family that moved around quite a bit, and Jim knew he put a lot of stock in having a steady job and a real place to come home to. But still, it took two. Everyone said that, and it was right. Brenda would have had to want to make things work, too, and any credit for a good relationship was at least half hers.

Jim figured that at the beginning, at least, every couple expected their marriage to last. Brenda and Ernie no doubt had; he and Elaine had; and Claude and LuAnn probably had. Some made it, and some didn't. Some relationships started out good and followed through, while others started out just as well and ended up on the rocks.

It was hard to tell, all right. He assumed he would get married again, some day, and he thought Dusty was the type of person he'd like it to be with, but he didn't know how either of them would be feeling even a month from now. Naturally he'd like to be sleeping with her, but he admitted to himself that things were better at their slow pace, at least for the time being.

Jim rolled onto his side. The rest of the camp was quiet, and he thought of the others sleeping out their troubles — or trying to — in the big open. Then he thought of the earth people they had met, the hostile pacifists who lived across country a ways. Maybe two miles away as the crow flew, those people were bedding down for the night in some arrangement or other. Jim gave a short, quiet laugh. It was funny how some people who just wanted peace of mind took the measures they did. People were the same, town and country alike. They would fight like hell with one another just to prove they wanted to be left alone. Life was full of contradictions, he had heard say, and whoever said that was right, too.

Claude was wearing his pistol again the next morning, which came as no surprise to Jim. Nothing had happened to cause him not to wear it. He had even explained to Jim that a sidearm was handy for finishing off an animal at close range once it was down, because a scope at close quarters was not accurate. Jim had nodded. It reminded him of the rationale he had once heard for driving a souped-up car: if the driver happened upon someone who had been in a wreck, he could get the victim to the hospital in short time, maybe. That was logic, Jim thought. Get a dangerous toy, and then look for chances to use it. A pistol-packer who kept an eye peeled for snakes in the mountains probably kept an ear tuned for burglars in the city.

Jim looked at Claude as he sat in the lantern light, blowing steam off his coffee. He imagined Claude in a Sacramento apartment, going to a window after hearing a noise in the night, then peeking through a curtain to see if it was Randy.

Claude and Ernie were talking about the morning hunt. Ernie said he thought they should try the same hunt as before.

"There's got to be deer in there," he said. "If there's deer anywhere, they're in there. I bet we walked right past 'em yesterday."

"We'll work it a little better," Claude said. "Maybe one of us should go down in and kick 'em out."

Jim felt himself cringe. Being the extra hunter, he was the logical choice to be the bird dog, and he didn't like the idea of being the one to make noises for someone like Claude to get ready to shoot at.

"Nah," Ernie said. "Your uncle Cal says the best way is to hunt 'em quiet, and I agree. If you get 'em stirred up, no one gets a shot. Not a good one, anyway."

"Then we'll hunt it the same way?"

"I think so. How 'bout you, Jim?"

Jim nodded, thinking he would just as soon be one ridge farther away.

Day was breaking as they climbed out of the pickup. Ernie and Claude walked away together, and Jim headed for the ridge he had walked the morning before. He was sure there would be less action there, as there were fewer trees and less cover for a deer to hide in, but he liked the openness and the solitude. He walked on, the long grass whispering against his pant legs, and an occasional bird lifting from the grass a few yards ahead of him.

The sun came up and turned the world from grey to yellow. Jim could hear the pickup in the north as Brenda drove back around to meet them at the bottom, and he heard a plane somewhere in the distance. A few minutes later he realized the pickup was stopped and the plane was out of hearing distance.

He walked slowly, stopping from time to time and scanning the grassy draw in front of him. The sun rose quite a ways in a short while, and the air warmed as the shadows drew shorter. Since there wasn't much to keep an eye on, Jim found it easy to think about other things. He imagined Claude over on the next ridge, studying the canyon and looking for an opportunity.

Jim felt his head making a slight shake. From the way Claude had been acting, Jim doubted he was working his way out of his mess like he said he was. He seemed mired in it, and it seemed like an unhealthy mess at that. Jim imagined Claude and his fellow bureaucrat, neckties loosened, having a beer in a downtown tavern after work. He imagined Claude keeping up the pretense as much as Randy did.

Then he imagined a scene with the man's wife — not as if Claude were there but as if he himself were, with a willing body in a dark room, and the grinning spirit of the husband stuck to him like a monkey on his back.

It gave Jim a shiver. That was damn sure a bad way to get tangled up. It he had a good feeling at all, it was in knowing it was Claude's problem and not his. Jim realized he could have ended up being hooked into something like that himself — maybe not that bad, but worse than he had been through. For as reckless as a fellow got when things went to pieces, it was just good luck he hadn't done worse.

Jim let out a weary sigh. He had been through a little bit as it was, and not so long ago. It seemed as if, for a while there, he had been looking at life through a pretty narrow tunnel — sort of like looking down the neck of a dark bottle. He remembered how obsessed he had been with just getting into the clinch with Arlene, as if one more exercise in covering the territory was going to solve anything. But the compulsion had been there, pulling him in, and it wasn't until quite a bit later that he could look back and see how little control he had had.

That must be the way it was with Claude, he imagined. Claude was full of confidence, always ready with an authoritative remark, but he was drawn in so deeply, pulled in so close to his problem, that he couldn't see what it looked like.

Jim thought it was like being down in a canyon. When a fellow got out on top he could see where he had come from and maybe how he had gotten there. But when he was down in there, he couldn't see much more than he could if he had his head stuck in a manzanita bush.

Jim took a deep breath and let it out. Every guy had to get through it on his own, it seemed like. Paddle your own canoe, saddle your own horse — call it one thing or another, it was something a fellow had to do himself.

The sun was warm now, and still climbing. Jim could feel it as he stepped out of the shade. He looked at the sun, and then he looked in back of him. He had heard it was a good habit to look in back from time to time, so he gave a backward glance when he thought of it. He had never gotten a deer that way, but he believed it was a good idea.

Jim imagined he was a little more than an hour into the hunt when he heard a shot.

He waited for a second shot but heard none. As Ernie had said before, one shot was a good sign. Jim stood still, listening. Then he heard the faint exchange of voices, what he imagined to be Claude and Ernie calling out to one another across their canyon. A hunter didn't call out unless the deer was down, Jim thought. He decided to walk over and take a look, figuring he could either help drag the deer or carry rifles as the other two did the dragging.

He came to Claude's ridge, which he recognized from having hunted it himself. He sidehilled until he reached the top, and then he searched the country below him, looking for the other hunters. He saw them up the canyon a ways, back to the right and across from him, more than halfway down the slope on Ernie's side. They were both leaning over a deer.

Jim began picking his way down the steep side of the draw. Judging from the location of the kill, he imagined Claude had taken the shot. That was fine. Everyone wanted to get a deer, and if you were the lucky one, you didn't want anyone else to be jealous. So you trained yourself to be glad for the other person.

Jim went through the trees at the bottom and came out below the other hunters. As he walked up the slope he could hear them talking in low tones, so he waited until he was close until he spoke. "Looks like you had some luck."

Ernie stepped back with bloody hands. Claude was crouched uphill from the deer, holding back a hind leg, and the intestines were hanging out on the downhill side.

"Claude killed one," Ernie said.

"Nice one?"

Ernie gave a serious look. "Should be good eatin'."

As Jim came closer he could see the reason for Ernie's restraint. Claude had killed a spike.

Spikes were young deer in their second year, called spikes because they had their first set of antlers, which didn't fork. They were often still with their mothers, and they were the most careless deer of all. They were the easiest to kill and therefore tempting, but the regulations were black and white. A deer had to be a forked horn or better. Everyone knew how easy it was to make a mistake, to see a fork when there was really just one slick tine on each side. Everyone knew how careful a person had to be, to make sure there was a second point — enough to hang a ring on, as the saying went.

"His horns crossed in the scope," Claude said. "He looked like a fork."

Jim nodded. It could happen, just as it did in the other stories, where there was water on the scope, or a dead branch in back of the deer's head.

"We sure don't just leave it here," Ernie said, leaning back in to finish the job of field dressing.

Jim let out a breath. "I guess not." He looked at Claude.

"I can take it back in the trunk of my car. I doubt that anyone will check me." Claude moved his head up and down, as if he had solved the problem.

"Made a good shot," Ernie said. "Right through the heart and lungs."

Claude leaned over to look. "Uh-huh."

When Ernie had the job finished, he and Claude each took an antler and began dragging. Jim had meanwhile slung his own rifle across his back, with the sling across his chest. Now he picked up the other two rifles and carried them. He walked ahead, having decided to get to the pickup first, leave off the rifles, and come back to help drag.

As he walked, he found himself irritated at Claude. Anyone could make that mistake, but a person who did brought the other members of the party into it — especially Ernie, who was into it up to his elbows. Jim realized he didn't have room to say much, though, as he himself had poached a deer before the season had even started. Still, that was different. Shooting something in the back yard was more discreet, and it didn't automatically implicate someone else.

When they got the deer to the pickup, Claude wondered out loud whether he should punch his tag for an illegal deer. "There's not even enough of a fork to keep it from sliding off," he said.

Jim could see how the tag would slip right off if Claude tied it the way most hunters did, wrapped around the antler beam.

"You could tie it around a hock," Ernie said. "That's the way they do it in those out-of-state places, where they shoot does and all."

Claude seemed to hesitate, then said, "I guess so. Hell, I'm done hunting anyway." He looked at Brenda, who gave him a pained smile.

Ernie and Jim took a little hunt after that and were back in camp before noon. Brenda and Claude had the tent packed up and waiting, the deer hanging from a pine tree, and the pickup washed out. After a short lunch, the group finished breaking camp. For the last item, Ernie and Claude laid the deer in a folded blue plastic tarp and set it in the back of the pickup bed. Then the group rolled out of camp. When they came to the gate, Ernie and Claude lifted the bundle, tarp and all, into the trunk of the Monte Carlo.

"Not a drop," Ernie said, looking for blood.

Brenda had already said she would ride back with Claude, so Jim crawled into the pickup cab with Ernie. Brenda and Ernie's rifles hung in the gun rack, and Jim's was riding in a gun case in back. Everything was in order.

"You guys go ahead," Ernie called out. "Don't wait for us."

Claude and Brenda nodded, and then the gravel crunched as the Monte Carlo pulled out onto the road.

Ernie and Jim had a good ride home, with the music loud and the wind blowing in through the open windows. Jim was relieved when the beige-colored car dropped out of sight up ahead on the main highway, and they didn't see it again until the late afternoon when they pulled into Ernie's driveway.

What little gloom had hung over them earlier seemed gone now. The four of them unloaded all the gear and sorted it out, and Jim put his things in his pickup. As he said his good-byes, he shook Claude's hand.

"I'll be here another week," Claude said. "Maybe I'll give you a call during the week, and we'll go out and have a beer."

Jim said, "Sure," but as he said it he wondered if they really would, or if it was just the kind of talk designed to make people feel good, like going to Buzzard Roost.

CHAPTER 11

On Monday, after watering the trees at the gate, Jim called Mrs. Kraemer to ask about the horse named Babe. The lady told him the horse had been out on a trial basis but was probably coming back. She went on to say that if the horse did come back, she and her husband were simply going to sell it, because they couldn't have the horse coming and going like that. She told Jim he could call again on the following Monday to find out how things stood. Jim said he would do that.

The other thing he had it in his mind to do was to call Dusty. Because of her work schedule, Jim had to call her in the early afternoon. The conversation was short but pleasant, and he made a lunch date for Sunday.

Jim got back into the work on his place, finishing the fence work on his upper pasture and then going to work on the corrals around the barn. He had more or less forgotten about his agreement with Claude until Wednesday evening, when the telephone rang. Claude wanted to know if Jim would like to go out for a beer, and Jim said he would. They agreed to meet at the Buckhorn.

On his way into town, Jim swerved to miss a black-and-white form that was scuttling across the road. *Skunks in August*, he thought. That was the time when there seemed to be more of them out on the road. That, and a full moon — there were always more road kills of anything during a bright moon.

Once in town, Jim hung a right and geared down as he pulled onto Main Street. Most of the businesses were closed, and the bars were lit up. A few cars were nosed up to the curb diagonally in front of the No-Tell. Over the years Jim had noticed that a person had sort of an inventory of the cars in a small town, and he more or less knew if a car was local or from out of town. He had thought about that as he had been keeping an eye out for Brant's pickup. He didn't see the dark

Ford or its driver now, but he recognized Lyle Chrisman getting out of his Chevy Super Sport.

Now Chrisman was a different kind of duck. As far as Jim knew, he had performed one worthy act in his thirty-some years. The story was pretty well known and had become one more part of the local lore. One day, while Chrisman was standing in line at the One-Stop Market and holding a fifth of Ten High by the neck, the man in front of him had pulled out a flat little automatic and called for the cash in the till. As the clerk was dishing into the tens, Lyle brought the round bottle of Ten High to bear upon the base of the would-be robber's skull.

Since then, Jim thought, Chrisman had taken on a bit of a swagger, as if he had gone through all his former life with this act of fulfillment struggling to come to the surface. After that day — the day when fate had put the Ten High bottle in his hand, the robber beside him, and probably not much interference in his head — it was said that he sometimes had Ten High courtesy of the One-Stop Market.

Jim knew him as a lethargic, humorless sort, tall and slow and not very talkative. If he was going into the No-Tell, that was fine; it would be one less deadbeat in the Buckhorn.

Jim found Claude with his foot on the rail, rolling dice with the woman tending bar. Claude ordered Jim a beer, paid for it out of the money he had in front of him, and went on shaking dice. As Jim slid into his low-backed barstool, he thought Claude seemed in good spirits. He was wearing the cap from Scooter's Bar and Grill, and with the exception of the gold choker chain he was wearing around his neck, he seemed to fit right in with the Buckhorn crowd. After a few more slams of the dice cups the game was over, and Claude forked the woman a dollar.

"I'm sick of Willie Nelson," he said. "Play anything but him."

"Crystal Gayle?"

"Love her," he said, with about as much sincerity as Jim would expect him to show to a highway patrolman.

Then he turned to Jim. "Well, have you learned any manners?"

Jim had to think for a second, and then he laughed. "Nope. Still my clumsy old self."

"I'll tell you, it doesn't get any easier."

Jim looked at him with a frown.

Claude put up a hand. "No deep meaning. I just meant it was hard to please people, even when you try."

Jim nodded. "I'd go along with that."

As they drank and chatted for the next twenty minutes or so, Jim became aware of some tension developing at the end of the bar. One of the Royce brothers was in the bar, and he was needling the fellow next to him. They were at the end of the bar, around the corner from the long side where Jim and Claude sat, so Jim could see the front of both men.

The Royce brothers were big, strapping guys in their early thirties. They hauled hay and firewood and anything else that put muscle in their arms and money in their pockets. They both had bushy, light brown hair and bristly short beards. Jim didn't know the brothers apart, but he knew that the man at the end of the bar was one of them.

The man who was being badgered was a relative newcomer. Jim had seen him around town for the last two or three years. He looked about forty years old, with dark blonde hair which he combed straight back from his forehead and temples. Being a roughneck sort of a backhoe operator, he was no slouch; but he was obviously not a match for Royce, and he seemed to be taking a full dose of abuse.

All this time, Royce had been standing while the other man had been sitting, so Royce loomed over the smaller man, who in turn couldn't move away very easily because he was stuck on his stool.

Suddenly Royce stepped back from the bar, took a long drag on his cigarette, dropped it and made a motion as if

112

stepping on it, and then shot out his open hand and hit the other man in the back of the head. The man's hair bounced out from his head, and he lurched forward against the bar.

"Reed's gonna get his ass kicked," Claude said.

In the course of the conversation, Jim had gathered that Claude had been down to the Buckhorn every night, so it didn't surprise him that Claude knew the man's name. Nor did it surprise him that Claude seemed to care so little about what might happen.

Royce stood back with his arms at his side as Reed settled back into his stool, swivelled with his back to Royce, and stood on the floor. Never looking at Royce, he walked all the way around him and came down the bar to stand a few places to the left of Jim.

Jim watched him in the mirror as he reached across the bar, took a shot glass, and closed his fist around it. His hand disappeared from sight and then he must have thought better of his plan, because the hand came back up on the bar and left the shot glass there. Royce had turned around as if to watch the pool game, and Jim imagined he had not seen much of what Reed was up to.

Reed spoke to the woman in back of the bar, and she called out, "Danny, I don't wanta see any more of that, or I'll have to eighty-six ya."

Royce turned around and nodded with a firm mouth. Jim saw that he had a drink in his hand now.

The bartender said to Reed, "You can go back to your stool. He won't do anything. I know him, and he knows I don't stand for any of that crap."

Reed took the long way back to his stool, walking around the pool table and along the cue rack and coming in on the other side of his seat, where he had left his money, his cigarettes, and his drink. He was halfway into his seat when Royce set his drink on the bar and said something. Reed stepped back.

113

Royce moved into him with half a dozen quick punches, knocking him into the cue rack and rattling the sticks. Reed was still on his feet when the bartender's shrill voice stopped the action.

"Danny! I told you! Now you get the hell out, or I'm callin' the cops!"

Royce said something to Reed and walked out the back door of the bar.

Jim felt a queasy feeling in his stomach. It had been quick, raw, and ugly. He had known the Royce brothers had a reputation for that sort of thing, but he hadn't actually seen it before. Now he had. Danny Royce had done as he damn well pleased, and no one had done a thing.

Reed was sinking into his stool now, and he shook his head at something the bartender said. It looked as if blood was coming out of Reed's ear, and he had a dazed look to him, but he didn't seem to need any help.

Jim gave a low whistle. "What does a guy do to deserve that?"

Claude, who seemed unbothered, took a drink from his beer and said, "Not much, I guess."

Reed left the bar a short while later, and the atmosphere lightened up again. When Jim was drinking his third beer, Claude said, "Well, it's been a nice vacation."

Jim almost laughed. "Do you go back to work on Monday?"

"Yeah."

Jim sensed that Claude wanted to bring up his old topic, so he said, "Back with what's-his-name?"

Claude lowered his bottle from his mouth and nodded. "Yeah. Randy. My friend."

"You expect more trouble with him when you get back?"

"Who knows? The sonofabitch is so two-faced."

"So you guys just go to work every day, and act like nothing happened?"

Claude frowned. "More or less. I think he's been runnin' me down with the supervisor."

"Oh, really?"

"Yeah, I was gettin' funny vibes before I left."

Jim thought for a second. "Do you think you were acting any different? Maybe your supervisor was picking up on something."

Claude turned down his mouth and shook his head. "Nah. I haven't done anything different. I go to work and do my job. I'm not porkin' anyone else in the office, and I'm not talkin' shit with the boss."

"Well, you'd think the boss would see through it sooner or later."

"He might. But that won't change this guy's act."

"Oh?"

"Nah. I talked to her on the phone, to see what was brewin', and he's comin' up with new moves." Claude took a swallow of beer. "He says he's not gonna let her get a divorce, that it was all her fault, that I came between them, and on and on."

"What's his angle?"

"This is really petty, but it's part of it. He's been on her dental plan because it's a better plan, and he's had a lot of work done on his mouth, and I think he wants to ride that out. But mostly, I think he just wants to jerk her around, make her think he wants to get back together."

Jim gave a weary sigh. "Dental work. It comes down to that."

"Man, I'll tell you. There's a story for everything with this guy. She told me about one scene they had with some people they used to be friends with. They were out at a bar with this other couple, and Randy starts feelin' up the other woman. So when they get outside, the other guy slams him up against the building, and Randy starts blubbering, 'Hit me, hit me.' Then she breaks in and asks the guy not to, because of all the dental work."

Jim shook his head. "It just gets deeper and deeper with this guy."

"Really. I'd have busted up his mouth for him."

"You think so?"

"I don't know. Maybe I'm just saying that. Maybe if I had him slammed up against the wall and had her yammerin' in my ear, maybe I'd think that was enough. Hell, I don't know. It's bad enough bein' anywhere close to the guy, but then to have him ask you to punch him."

"Hard to say, huh?"

"Yeah, he's got a funny way of workin' you."

Jim sat through another beer with Claude, then let out a yawn and pleaded work the next day.

Claude said he was going back to Sacramento on Friday, but he would be back in town before long, and they could get together and do something.

Jim said fine.

On his way home, Jim thought it would probably be good for Brenda and Ernie if Claude went back to the city, where that sort of sick business belonged. That was what it seemed like — the kind of turmoil people went through in a city. Then on second thought, Jim supposed the same kind of thing could happen in a small town, if you got the right kinds of people together.

On Saturday, Jim went with Ernie to cut firewood. Ernie knew of a fellow who needed to pull out an almond tree to make room for a swimming pool. The man had waited until the nuts turned ripe, and then he wanted the tree out as soon as possible. Ernie, who always seem to know about someone who wanted to give away a pair of ducks or a rabbit or an expendable tree, had jumped at the chance.

"It's a nice tree," he told Jim as they pulled out onto the road from Ernie's place. "One of those old ones, with a trunk that's grown in a swirl."

Jim nodded. "Should be good firewood."

"No doubt," said Ernie. "Let it cure for six months, and it'll be great."

"Do we have to take out the trunk, too?"

"Nah. The guy that's gonna dig the pool will yank out the stump."

"That's handy."

"Yeah." Ernie shifted gears. "But I dug up an almond stump once. Big-ass stump, about a yard across. It was good and dead, but the roots were still hard. It took me all afternoon one winter day to dig it up — the ground was soft, so that helped. And you know, that was incredibly good wood. Even the roots."

"You dug it up yourself?" Jim knew Ernie was a little superstitious about cutting wood by himself. A cousin of his had died in the woods, by himself, when his chain saw gouged his leg. Jim remembered that story every time Ernie invited him along to cut wood.

"Oh, yeah," Ernie answered. "Just me and an ax, and a pick and shovel."

"Then you split it all up?"

"Yeah. I did that by hand, too. It was a bitch of a job. That one was one of those gnarly old trunks, too. Harder'n hell to split. Good wood, though."

When Jim saw the tree they were to cut down, he felt guilty. It still had green leaves on it. But it was fated, and that was all there was to it. Ernie could get the wood, or someone else could.

Ernie started by cutting down the four large branches that grew out of the main trunk. Jim went to work with a pair of pruning shears, trimming off the small growth so Ernie could then cut the branches into stove lengths. The chain saw kept up a steady whine, so Jim and Ernie didn't talk much until they took a mid-morning break.

"Did Claude go back to Sacramento?" Jim asked the question as he held a cup beneath Ernie's open thermos.

"Yeah. He left yesterday."

"So he could have the weekend to go on the prowl before he goes back to work?"

Ernie laughed as he poured himself a cup. "I guess."

"Did he get plenty of therapy like he said?"

"If you mean was he a pain in the ass and did he keep Brenda worried, yes. If you mean did he get his shit together, no." Ernie screwed the cap onto the thermos.

"I didn't think so."

Ernie gave the bored, disgusted look. "Whoever that woman was, she'd call him at all hours of the night, and he'd sit in the living room with just the hall light on, and he'd talk for an hour in a low tone of voice. Or he'd come in from the bar at two in the morning, and call her, and go through the same routine."

"Kept you up?"

"Not up, but awake. It's that kind of irritation you can't sleep through. And Brenda layin' there tied up in a knot, too."

"Why is she takin' it so rough?"

"It's her little baby brother." Ernie shook his head. "Ought to have his ass kicked, that's what I think."

Jim got back to his own place in the late afternoon. He was tired and sweaty, and he had debris in his hair and down his neck — dark little dried pieces of bark and twig, and light pieces of sawdust. He had drunk his half of a six-pack, so he felt lazy and listless. What he needed was a shower. He took off all his clothes on the back porch, went into the warm house, and took a shower. He had thought he might go into town tonight, just for the sights and sounds, but he decided he would stay home and take it easy. After all, he had a lunch date with Dusty for the next day, and he could wait until then for another sample of the outer world.

As he sat in his armchair in the living room, he remembered the clean, smooth stump of the almond tree they had cut down. It was too bad, he thought, but a tree didn't have a chance against a swimming pool. A few years back, Hardesty the insurance agent had had one of the biggest oak trees in town taken down, and it wasn't even in the way of the pool he was putting in. He had it cut down because the cleanup of the leaves would have been too much bother.

Jim remembered stories he had heard when he worked for the walnut and prune grower — how it had taken a crew of men to clear out an old grove of oak trees so the farmer could put in the walnut orchard. They had to blast out the stumps and haul them away in dump trucks with all the trunks and branches. There was even a story about one guy who had gotten killed by setting his powder charges wrong.

Big oak trees, Jim had been told. But they were in the way.

Well, he thought, at least a walnut orchard had taken their place. That was better than a swimming pool.

On Sunday morning, Jim got a call from Ernie. "Well, it sounds like Brenda's brother Claude got himself into a real jackpot."

"Oh, really? What kind?"

"He's in the hospital. He got a bullet put through him."

"Is he all right?"

"I think so. Brenda and her mom are on their way down there right now."

Jim felt the sick feeling in his stomach again. "What happened? Did he get tangled up with that guy Randy that he told me about?"

"We don't know yet. He was downtown, where the hookers and hoodlums hang out, and someone put a bullet through his ribs."

"Did he have his pistol with him?"

"I don't know. I think he's just damn lucky it wasn't any worse."

"Sounds like it. What the hell was he doin' down in that part of town, anyway?"

119

"I don't know that, either. Maybe just living too close to the edge, like you said before."

"I suppose there'll be an explanation come out of it."

Ernie let out a breath. "Oh, I imagine we'll hear some kind of story."

"Boy, what a mess."

"You're tellin' me. He's put Brenda through a lot of worry. I'd like to kick his ass for it, but that's not a nice thing to say right now."

"No, I guess not."

"My theory is, if his old man had kicked his ass a little more when he was little, he'd be better at stayin' out of trouble."

Jim felt himself make a face. "The way he tells it, all this trouble came lookin' for him."

"Well, we both know Claude."

"You know him better than I do."

"Yeah, but you know, there's more than one side to every story. And we'll hear his side to this one."

"I suppose there'll be a police report, too."

"Oh, yeah."

Jim paused and then said, "I hope everything works out all right. I mean, I hope he isn't too bad off, and I hope Brenda gets through it okay."

"Yeah, she will. He just pisses me off, though."

"Well, don't say anything you wish you hadn't."

"Yeah, I know." Ernie laughed and then paused. "Well, I'd better get off the phone. It'll be jangling for the rest of the morning. You have a good day, Jim."

"I hope to. I'm having lunch with Dusty."

"I'm glad to hear that. It makes me downright happy, in the middle of all this other grief. I hope you have a good time. She's a good girl, Jim."

"I know. Thanks, Ernie. Take care."

CHAPTER 12

Jim and Dusty went to lunch at La Campaña, a Mexican restaurant on the old highway. In the days before the freeway, the place had been a steakhouse with some seafood dishes, but with the redistribution of traffic and business, The Golden Bull had closed its doors and gone out of existence. A couple of years later the place was reopened as La Campaña, which struggled at first but eventually held on and became a fixture in the valley. Because it had a location between two towns, it attracted people from both. It had also acquired a reputation for being genuine, so college people from fifty miles away had discovered it. On Friday and Saturday evenings the place was packed with farm country folks, professorial couples, and student groups of ten or more. But on Sundays a person could get a table without having to wait, and since Dusty preferred not to go out to eat in the place where she worked or in places very much like it, she was happy to go to La Campaña.

Dusty looked fresh and well-rested as she sat across the table from Jim. Her light-colored hair, full-bodied and clean, hung loosely to her shoulders. She was wearing a beige-colored blouse, and her hazel eyes looked greener than usual.

A pretty Mexican girl about sixteen years old took their order, and when they were alone again, Dusty began a story.

"I heard this from Dean Hazens," she said. "You know he comes in to eat pretty often since he lost his wife. Well, you know he raises alfalfa."

"Oh, sure. I used to buy hay from him."

Dusty nodded and paused, as if she was making the connection, and then she continued. "Well, he said he got a call from one of his neighbors, and as soon as I tell the rest of the story you'll know who it was. Anyway, since it hasn't been a

121

very good year for alfalfa, the prices are up, and no one has a big surplus because it's all bought up."

"Sure," Jim said. "A lot of it was bought last winter, six months before the first cutting."

"Right. And of course these neighbors have all of theirs sold, and their daughter is getting married next week."

"Oh, okay. Now I know who you mean." Jim smiled.

"So they're going to have the reception at their house, and the lady wants to put on a good impression."

"Uh-huh."

"And she wants to borrow a couple of truckloads of hay, just to fill up the front of their barn, so everyone will think they've got a barn full of hay."

Jim shook his head as he smiled. "Just so their guests will think they're doing better than anyone else in a bad year. What did Dean tell her?"

"He said his hay was all sold, but she had seen he still had some in a stack. She said all she wanted to do was borrow it, and nothing would happen to it. But he said it was sold, and it wasn't his to loan out."

Jim laughed. "Some people will do just about anything to make a good impression. She probably didn't like getting turned down."

Dusty smiled, and her eyes sparkled green. "Probably not. And like Dean said, anyone else who would care how much hay these people had in their barn would probably know if they had any left, anyway. They weren't going to fool anyone."

"That's right," Jim said. "I worked for a guy that always knew when one of his neighbor's milk cows had died. He'd see the tallow truck drive in there, and then he'd quit what he was doing until he heard the boom of the dead cow when it dropped in the back of the truck. Then he'd laugh and go back to work."

Dusty laughed. "It's just like in town, isn't it?"

Jim felt a tinge of embarrassment, but then he realized she wasn't including him in her criticism. If there was a joke to be made about someone else's dirty laundry, Dusty was inviting Jim to join in the laughter. That was a good sign; it meant they were past the point at which she might feel she had to tip-toe around that sort of topic.

Their meal came. Dusty had chicken tacos, and Jim had chile verde. They both drank Seven-Up out of amber-colored plastic glasses, and Jim had a wholesome feeling about the event.

As they ate, Dusty asked him about the hunting trips he had recently taken.

Jim explained that he had been out on two separate weekends and that someone else in the party had gotten a deer each time.

"That's good," she said.

Jim tore a flour tortilla in half. "Oh, do you like venison?"

She nodded.

"Have you ever been out on anything like that?"

"Oh, yeah," she said. "I've hunted."

"Really? I didn't know that."

She raised a napkin to her mouth and then set it down. "With my dad and brothers. When they weren't doing their man thing, like they did on opening weekend when they didn't have any women in camp, they'd let me go along."

It seemed to Jim that she spoke of it as if it were way in the past, even though she wasn't that old. He knew her father had been dead for a couple of years, so he imagined she looked back on that time as a closed chapter. "Did you ever shoot one?" he asked.

She was about to take a bite on her taco, and she paused. "One. The only one I ever shot at."

"Well, that's good."

"My dad drilled it into my head not to take a bad shot. So I hunted for four seasons and took one shot."

They each resumed eating until Jim asked, between bites, "Do you ever think you'd like to go out and try your hand at it again?"

"Oh, yeah. But my brothers are off and gone now, and they probably wouldn't invite me anyway. That was always my dad's doin's, I think, to bring me along."

Jim thought for a second. "Early season isn't even over yet, and there's a late season after that. It's shorter, but it still lasts three weeks or so."

"That's what we always hunted, was the later season."

Jim nodded. That must have been why she had seemed surprised when he had first told her the season was about to open. "Well," he said, "it's something to think about."

He took a quick look at her as she used her fork to pick up some of the dropped pieces of taco. It occurred to him that there was a lot more to Dusty than he realized — not just because he had learned that she hunted, but because it showed him he really knew very little about her. Then he pin-pointed where some of the good feeling of the moment came from; it came from learning something new about her. If that in itself made him happy, then things were on a good track.

At lunch time on Monday, Jim dialed Mrs. Kraemer's number again to ask about the horse. The lady said Babe had been returned and was for sale, and Jim was welcome to come out and take a look. Jim said he would do that.

As soon as Jim saw Babe, he remembered Mrs. Kraemer's earlier comment about the horse being "so different." The horse had a mottled, blue roan coat with specks and blotches of darker color against a blue-grey background. She had a pink nose, a pink eyelid on the left side, and a cream-colored white circle around the left eye. She also had an off-white patch on her chin. The middle of the horse's back was on a level with Jim's shoulder, which seemed about right.

He moved closer to the horse, and she moved her head toward him. He approached her left shoulder, patted her on the neck, then ran his hand across her withers, down behind her shoulder, and onto her chest. He hadn't been around horses very much, but he had been around plenty of animals, including hundreds of milk cows bigger than Babe. As he patted with his right hand, he kept his left hand on the top of her shoulder so he could feel any sudden movements.

Babe was a calm animal, all right. She didn't seem to be bothered at all. Jim moved around in front of her, ducking beneath her head and neck, keeping his right hand resting against her. He stood by her right shoulder and then went through the motions he had gone through on the other side, patting and brushing with his left hand this time as he kept his right hand against the horse.

Jim could feel the heat of the sun on the horse's coat, and he could smell the horse smell that had always been agreeable to him. Babe had been eating alfalfa hay, and the sweet smell of chewed hay mixed with the smell of sweat and hair and dust. It all seemed familiar and comforting. He knew that some horses could be dangerous, but he felt an immediate confidence with Babe. He crossed in front of her again and moved into her, with his left arm beneath her neck and his right hand up on her withers, where he patted with enough pressure to raise a tiny cloud of dust.

"She's very gentle," said Mrs. Kraemer. "Our daughter and all her friends rode her, sometimes two or three of them at a time, bareback."

Jim looked at her and nodded. He had bought enough animals to know not to seem enthusiastic right away. He leaned down to brush the front leg and to see if the animal had any quirks, and Babe lifted her hoof. He took it and held it, sensing that the horse expected him to.

"She's real easy to work on, too," Mrs. Kraemer said. "She does need to have her hooves trimmed, of course."

Jim noticed that the hoof wall was grown out irregularly and chipped. He set the foot down and moved to the hind quarter of the horse. Standing at the horse's hip, he patted the round part and then moved down the leg to the hock. With a little nudging he got Babe to give him the hind foot, too. He looked at it and set it down, then crossed in back of the horse, keeping his left forearm against the hind end. He moved on up the right side of the horse, and he smiled when he saw her head turned and her dark right eye watching him.

"We've got the saddle and all if you'd like to ride her."

Jim hesitated. He thought he would look foolish if he let her saddle the horse, and if he did it himself, he might be seen doing something that wasn't up to code. And besides, he wouldn't know anything more about the horse if he did ride it — except perhaps whether it was going to throw him off or not.

"That's all right," he said. "You say she's gentle. If your daughter and her friends rode her, that's a pretty good indication." He smiled at Mrs. Kraemer. "I sort of like the horse."

Mrs. Kraemer smiled back. "Well, she's for sale."

They talked about terms. Mrs. Kraemer was a little firmer about the actual price than Jim had thought she might be, but she said she didn't have to have it all at once. She told Jim he could have the horse, the saddle, the bridle, a halter, a blanket and pad, and a bucketful of brushes and combs for seven hundred dollars. She said her husband could deliver the horse with the neighbor's horse trailer.

Jim thought about it for a moment. He knew that on the current market, a horse like this one was worth four to five hundred dollars. The tack was probably worth two and a half. He liked Babe, but the old business instinct was coming back to save him. He offered Mrs. Kraemer six hundred dollars on the spot for just the horse, the saddle, and the bridle.

She hesitated, then told him he could have the whole works for six-fifty.

He knew she didn't have any use for the little stuff, and he knew he wouldn't be able to buy it for fifty dollars anywhere else, so he agreed to her price. He wrote her a check and gave directions to his place. She told him to expect Babe that evening.

As Jim drove his pickup back north along the river road, he figured any money he had saved by firing Brant was gone now. Then he remembered the old line that the horse trader tells the greenhorn as he slaps him on the shoulder. "Mister, you just bought yerself a horse." It was still a funny joke.

That evening the husband delivered Babe as promised. When the pickup and horse trailer had rattled out of the yard and on down the hill, Jim went to the corral and looked at the horse. She had her nose in the trough and the pink eye looking his way. As he approached her, she lifted her head; her nostrils widened, and water dripped from her white chin. Jim smiled. It was nice to have an animal around. Now he didn't live alone any more.

After looking in the newspaper with no success, Jim imagined that the best place to find out about a horseshoer would be in one of the bars. He decided to go to town on Tuesday evening. Out of a sense of caution he avoided the Trail's End. He thought of going to the Buckhorn, but he recalled the ugly scene he had witnessed the last time he had been there. He considered going to the No-Tell, but then he remembered the last time he had been in that place.

A tall, flabby bartender with broad shoulders and a broader girth, with a loose silky shirt hanging down, had stood by the trash can and drained a can of Coors down his throat. Then in one swift downward stroke he had flung the empty can into the trash, where it crunched onto the other empties. Jim had been in the bar long enough to see the bartender do it three times, and he had found the man's air of authority to be repugnant. The No-Tell was a low-class place to begin with, where half the patrons drank Coors in a can, but that vignette had been the kicker. Jim decided to go to the Buckhorn after all.

The woman who had been tending bar the last time was on duty again. She served Jim without much comment and left him to look at himself in the mirror. Jim stayed long enough to drink two beers and to talk to a couple of fellows he knew. The man to talk to, they said, was Roger King.

Jim was getting ready to make an exit with his acquired knowledge when an image in the mirror gave him a start. He saw a head of dark brown hair, the profile of eyebrows and nose, the glow of colored light on the texture of a face that registered before he turned and saw the person.

Arlene had her purse on her shoulder, and she looked as trim and ready to go as always. "I saw your pickup outside, so I thought I'd come in and say hi."

Jim smiled and nodded. He knew it would be impolite to give her the brush-off. It would be the equivalent of saying all she'd ever been good for was sex, and now he didn't want any. Even if that was true, it was no way to treat a woman. "Buy you a drink?" he said.

"Thanks, sailor." She smiled at him through lowered lashes.

Jim ordered her a drink but none for himself, as he had a little beer left in his bottle. Silence hung in the air between them as they waited for her drink. Then she spoke.

"What have you been doing?"

"Oh, workin', mostly." He thought for a second and then added, "Been on a couple of huntin' trips."

"Do any good?"

He shook his head.

"I haven't heard of many people who have."

"Neither have I," he said.

Her drink arrived, he paid for it, and she thanked him.

She used the red straw to sip from the drink. "You don't get around much these days, do you?"

"Not much." Jim had turned to her and was sitting on the edge of his stool with his left foot touching the floor.

Arlene was standing facing him, but she hadn't moved close. "I thought maybe you didn't want to call me." She bent to her drink again and gave him an upward glance.

Jim thought she was making a veiled reference to Brant, so he said, "Not so much that."

"Aw, go on," she said. "You're practically married."

Now Jim understood the other possible reference. It was delivered in the form of a challenge, and it sparked the old urge. He could feel it come up inside him, as if he was poised again with his fist over the bucket of grease. He made himself turn to the bar and pick up his beer. Then he swivelled back and said, "Not really." The surge was subsiding. "I'm just trying to keep things uncomplicated."

She smiled and took another sip on her drink. Jim wished she would say something, and then she did. "That's up to you."

He shrugged.

"Well, I came in to say hello, that's all. I didn't want you to think you couldn't talk to me." She looked at him, and the challenge was gone.

Maybe she had tried it and was being nice enough not to push it. Maybe she was referring to Brant and Dusty both at that moment.

"No," he said, shaking his head, "I wouldn't think that."

"That's good." She set her glass on the bar. "I didn't really want a drink, but I thank you for it. I just went out to the store for a couple of things, and my kids are waiting for me at home."

Jim set his beer on the bar and offered his hand in friendship. She returned the gesture, and he knew her hand was cold only because she had been holding a Seven-and-Seven.

When Jim got home he looked up Roger King's number, but he decided not to call until the next day. He thought it was a little late in the evening to be calling someone he didn't know that well. The next morning, he preferred to go right to work as usual, so he waited until noon to make his call. He dialed Roger's number and talked to his wife, who said Roger was out at his property. Jim said he knew where it was. He thanked her and hung up.

Roger lived in a rundown house in town with his wife and three kids, who looked very much as Roger had looked when he was a boy. Jim remembered him as having uncombed hair, loose-fitting clothes, and bad teeth. He had dropped out of high school and had hung around town, picking up seasonal work hauling hay and doing ranch work. In his own way he was industrious, and he had acquired a five-acre parcel out on the west side, between Jim's place and town but a little farther south where the ground was poor and gravelly.

In the heat of early afternoon, Jim drove down the road toward Roger's place. As he drew nearer, he saw two dark-colored horses standing head to tail in the little pasture. There were no shade trees in the field, and the horses stood out in the open, swishing their tails to keep the flies off one another. At the front corner of the property Jim saw Roger's orange Dodge pickup parked in front of an old silver Airstream trailer.

Jim pulled in and parked behind Roger's pickup. The door to the trailer was open, and as Jim got out of his vehicle he saw Roger appear at the doorway. Roger waved and motioned him forward, then moved back inside the trailer.

As Jim put his foot onto the metal step of the trailer, he saw that there were two people sitting at the table in the front end. The interior of the trailer was dark, and at first Jim thought the other man was Brant.

"Come on in, Jim," Roger said in a loud voice.

Jim stepped inside, and as his eyes adjusted he saw that the other man was Roger's brother Norman. He and Roger each had a can of Pabst sitting on the table in front of them, and smoke curled up from two cigarettes in a black plastic ashtray. Jim said hello to both men, and since neither of them made a move forward to shake hands, he just stood there with his thumbs in his pockets.

Roger grinned. "Hot sumbitch out there."

Jim smiled. "Sure is."

"Care for a beer?" Norman asked.

"No, thanks."

Norman smiled as he lifted his cigarette to his mouth. "We got plenty."

"That's all right. Thanks, though." Jim looked around and saw that the trailer had wood paneling and cabinets. "This is a nice old outfit," he said.

"Sure is," Roger said. "I bought this at an auction for two hundred dollars. Can you believe that?" He took a drag of his cigarette and blew out a stream of smoke.

Jim shook his head.

"Sure you don't want a beer?" Roger asked.

"No, thanks."

"Well, then, you must have come out here for some other reason. Everyone else comes out to drink beer." Roger grinned, and so did Norman.

Jim looked at the two of them. He hadn't told anyone yet that he had a horse, and he realized he felt shy at bringing up the topic in front of two people at once. "Well," he said, "I got a horse, and I need someone to trim its hooves."

Roger wrinkled his left nostril and said, "Just a trim? He doesn't have any shoes on him?"

"Well, it's a she, but no, she doesn't have any shoes."

"What are you gonna do with her?"

Jim gave him a questioning look.

"I mean, are you just gonna ride her, or are you gonna take her up in some rough country?" He gave Jim a sidelong look. "You don't rope, do you?"

"Nah, I just plan to ride her a little bit. Up on my place, you know." Jim motioned with his head in the direction of his own place.

Roger nodded. "You don't need no shoes out there. But if you take her into any rocky country, you'll want shoes."

"Uh-huh." Jim looked from Roger to Norman. It looked as if they were into a relaxed afternoon. He looked back at Roger and asked, "Is that the kind of thing you can do?"

"Oh, yeah."

"When do you think you could do it?"

Roger tapped his cigarette in the ash tray. "Oh, some time this evening, if that's all right with you. Best time to do that kind of work is in the morning or evening, when it's cool."

"This evening would be fine. You know where I live nowadays, don't you?"

"Oh, yeah."

"Well, I'll look forward to seeing you this evening, then." Jim nodded to the two brothers, who nodded back, and then he walked out into the blazing afternoon. The steering wheel and gearshift and even the keys were hot to his touch as he gunned up the engine and backed out onto the road.

Later that afternoon, Jim called Dusty and asked if she might like to come out to his place for dinner. She said it sounded like a nice idea, and they agreed on Thursday

132

evening. Then, just before they hung up, Jim told her he had gotten a horse named Babe. He heard delight in Dusty's voice as she repeated the name and said she couldn't wait to meet her.

Roger showed up that evening by himself. He parked the orange Dodge in the shade of the sycamore tree and got out. His voice sounded clear and steady as he said, "If you bring her out here to the tailgate, I can work on her."

Jim brought Babe out on a halter and lead rope, and he stood facing her as Roger went to work. He strapped on a pair of leather chaps, took a long pair of nippers out of his wooden tool tray, and went to Babe's left front foot. With his back to Jim he picked it up and pulled it through his legs, where he held it in a crouch as he nipped off a ring of old hoof. He dropped that foot and went under the horse's neck to the other front foot, picked it up, and trimmed it in the same way. Then he moved to the right rear and the left rear, and ended up where he had started. He set the nippers in the tool box and took out a long rasp. Then he reached for a metal tripod, which he set in front of Babe's front foot. He lifted her lower leg and set the hoof onto the peak of the tripod, and then he rasped the hoof smooth all the way around.

"She's pretty good about it," he said as he picked up the foot and let it drop to the ground.

"Uh-huh."

Roger finished the other three hooves as he had done the first one. The whole operation had taken him less time than it would have taken to drive out from town. When Jim asked him how much, he said, "Ten dollars."

As Jim dug out the money, Roger tossed his things back into the pickup. "That should do 'er," he said. "Call me in six or eight weeks, or sooner than that if her feet start lookin' chipped." Then he was rumbling out of the yard in the orange pickup.

Jim stood with the lead rope coiled in his left hand as he patted Babe on the neck with his right. "You look just fine," he said. "You're ready for company."

CHAPTER 13

On Thursday, Jim went to work planning and fixing dinner for his guest. With all the produce in season he made a good haul at the market and put together a respectable salad. He also baked a couple of potatoes. For the main course he floured and fried some venison steaks, then made a gravy and cooked the steaks a little longer in that.

Although he wasn't much of a connoisseur of wine, he knew enough not to buy Gallo or any of the other wines with metal caps. That was wino stuff, regardless of how the company was trying to re-create its image. He had bought a liter and a half of Almaden claret, and as he set it on the table he remembered Claude's story about the Algerian wine. He smiled as he shook his head. The last he had heard, Claude was on the mend. The story behind his getting shot was yet to come, but the first spell of worry had passed. Now Jim could laugh at the story of the cheap wine and the rotten hangovers. This claret should be all right, he thought. It wasn't cheap, and it wasn't something to show off. It was just some decent wine to drink with a venison dinner.

When Dusty showed up she looked fresh and healthy, as she had on Sunday. Her hair was loose and full, and her eyes had a sparkle. She was dressed in a light yellow, short-sleeved blouse, a pair of denim shorts, and leather sandals. She was carrying a double-crust pie in a glass dish.

"You've got a nice view," she said.

"Thanks. I was hoping you might get to see it." He cleared a space on the counter. "You can set it here," he said, moving aside. "What kind is it?" He leaned to smell it, and most of what he could smell was cinnamon.

"Pear."

"Really?" He straightened up and looked at her. "Pears, like Bartlett pears?"

She nodded. "My mom had a whole box of Lake County pears, and they were all turning ripe on her at once."

"Well, that's nice. I don't think I've ever had a pear pie."

"I'm sure you'll like it."

Jim hesitated. "Did you make it?"

She let out a short laugh. "Of course I did."

"Well, then I know I'll like it."

Jim adjusted the burner beneath the frying pan, turning it to the lowest flame he could. He didn't want to serve dinner the minute she walked through the door, so he thought he would let the steaks simmer in the gravy a few minutes more.

He looked up and smiled at Dusty.

"Well," she said, "will there be time for me to see your horse before the sun goes down?"

Jim glanced at the flame he had just lowered. "Sure. We could go right now. Then we wouldn't feel we had to hurry through dinner."

She smiled. "That's good. I've been wanting to meet Babe."

The sun was slipping in the west, but the evening air was still warm as they walked across the driveway to the barn and corral.

Jim glanced at her sandals. "Do you want to go into the corral?" he asked.

"Sure," she said.

Jim slid the board latch on the gate, and the two of them went into the pen. Babe came up to them, and Dusty moved forward. With her right hand she patted Babe's neck, and with her left she scratched the front of Babe's throat, between the jaws and in back of the chin.

Dusty turned and smiled at Jim. "I like her."

Jim nodded. "She's just fine."

They stood in the corral for a few minutes, and then they left Babe by herself as they went back into the house.

Jim put the biscuits in the oven and set the rest of the meal on the table. "We can serve ourselves," he said. "Let me put on some music." He had two records of Spanish guitar music, so he put one of them on to play. Then he and Dusty sat down to dinner. A few minutes later, the bell went off on the timer, so Jim got up and pulled the biscuits out of the oven. He scooted them onto a plate and set them in front of Dusty.

"These biscuits are all right," she said, after buttering one and biting into it.

He had cracked them out of a tube and had been afraid they might seem tacky amidst the rest of the food, which was all original, so he had halfway apologized. "Not bad," he said now, tasting the one he had buttered for himself. "I'd like to be able to make my own biscuits, but I haven't gotten around to it yet."

"It's pretty easy," she said, "but these are fine."

"I'm probably a pretty typical guy," he went on. "Cook on top of the stove. If I bake anything, it's a potato."

She looked at him. "Girls just grow up learning those things. But a lot of men know how."

"Sure, like cooks. Restaurant cooks."

She smiled. "Or bachelors."

He smiled back, appreciating her use of the word "bachelor." He didn't use the word to describe himself because he associated it with never having been married, but he thought she used the word without hesitation.

"It seems like a lot of trouble to cook something in the oven for just one person," he said.

Her eyes twinkled. "That's the best way. Because your first few batches of biscuits are likely to turn out too hard or too heavy, till you get the hang of it."

He laughed. "Thanks for the warning."

They ate for a few minutes without speaking, and Jim had a sense of something he often felt but necessarily kept to himself. It was the sense of being divorced. Sometimes he choked on the "D" word, and in its stead he had developed the phrase "living on my own again." But the bare fact persisted, and it was a stigma, as if he had made a public announcement that he had a flaw, that he had failed at something really important, that a relationship with him would be a big risk. The sense of being divorced was what he had heard some people call "baggage"; they said that in a future relationship a person needed to find someone who had the same amount of baggage. It made sense, but it also made sense to be drinking wine and talking about biscuits with someone who had never been married. At least, it seemed normal at the moment.

"Is this some of this year's deer?" she asked.

He saw no reason to doctor the truth. "Um, yes, it is." He paused. "Home grown."

She looked at him with a question on her face.

He felt himself suppressing a smile. "I took the liberty of protecting my property. Technically, a little before the season opened."

She raised her eyebrows and stuck her knife and fork into a piece of steak. "Tastes fine."

"Thanks."

She laughed. "I'm sorry. I was taught not to ask questions like that. You know, like, 'When did you shoot this pheasant, Uncle Bob?' So it just seemed kind of funny when I muffed it."

Jim laughed. "No problem here."

After a little while Dusty said, "I like your horse."

Jim smiled. "Thanks. I think she's going to be all right."

"I didn't notice any other animals. Do you not have any dogs or cats?"

Jim raised his eyebrows. "I haven't been up here that long. I'm still getting settled in, I guess. I suppose I'll get a cat or two, to keep down the mice. And I would like to get a dog." He thought, then asked, "Do you like cats and dogs?"

"I like dogs better," she said, "but cats are all right. I don't like them in the house. My father said he had an aunt who used to let the cat get up on the table and lick the butter, and he was thoroughly disgusted by that, so we never had cats in the house."

Jim almost laughed, remembering how Brenda and Ernie let their dog, Sam, lick the plates. "You like dogs, though?"

"Oh, yeah."

"So do I. When I get ready to look for one, I'll let you know."

She nodded. "This would be a good place for a dog."

After dinner they set the dishes in the sink and went to sit in the living room. Jim put on the second record of guitar music, then brought the wine from the kitchen and set it on the end table. He sat down next to Dusty, and she held up her glass to touch his.

Moonlight streamed in through the living room window as Jim and Dusty sat together on the couch. He had shut off the lights when he got up to turn the record over, and now they sat cozy. He had kissed her but briefly a few times before this evening, and even though he sensed that the occasion might be more opportune at the present, he didn't want to ruin anything by being too forward. With the two fingers of his left hand he touched the back of her hand, her upper arm, the side of her neck. The moon was at half-moon or a little past, so there was enough light in the room for him to see her smile as he made his small gestures.

When the record had finished playing, the two of them sat for a while without saying anything. Although the windows were open to let in the cool evening air, no noises came from the outside.

"This is nice," she said. "Calm and quiet."

"Uh-huh. A person almost gets to taking it for granted, he gets so used to the peacefulness."

They sat for a couple of more minutes without talking until Jim spoke again. "You know, this is a good way to do things."

"In what way do you mean it?"

He realized he had been speaking from his thoughts, as if she had been following them. "I mean, just getting to know each other, little by little."

She looked straight ahead as she said, "Well, it's not something you can do all at once."

"No, you're right. And even if you've known someone for a long time, it's different if you want to get to know them, you know, personally, or in a different way than just saying hello on the street."

"Uh-huh."

"But I guess I meant, it was good not rushing into anything."

She looked at him and nodded.

"And I hope I'm not putting my foot in my mouth, but, I mean, I assume — or I guess I hope, anyway, that there's some mutual interest."

Dusty's hand turned upward on her lap as she said, "Oh, yeah."

"I don't know," he said. "It seems like a funny thing to even be talking about, but I just wanted to say it — that I thought things were going all right." He held up his wine glass, and she touched hers to his.

They sat a little closer now, but he had not put his arm around her. He imagined they were both thinking about what should come next.

After a few minutes Dusty spoke, with the tone of having something she wanted to go at deliberately. "When I was younger," she said, "about fifteen or sixteen, I used to read Ann Landers every day."

"Uh-huh."

"It seemed like it was such a good way to learn a lot about life out in the world." She paused for a second. "Even though, you know, you hear the stories that the letters are all fake, just for set-ups, so she can talk about everything she wants to talk about."

"I've heard that, but not from anyone who would actually know."

"Really," she said, with a short laugh. Then after a brief silence she went on. "But I remember reading one piece of advice that she gave, and whether the letter was hokey or not, it didn't matter, because the advice seemed so — dependable."

"Uh-huh."

"This lady had written in, and she said she was getting serious with this man, and he had proposed to her, and she had accepted, and then she wondered if she should tell him she had been married before."

"Boy, that seems like a pretty major thing not to have told him by then."

"It does, doesn't it? But when I was that young, the people in the letters always seemed so much older, and this one seemed so normal, like it was the type of situation that happened to a lot of people."

There was a pause as if to let him speak, so Jim said, "For all I know, maybe it is pretty common. But either way, I would guess she told the lady to come clean."

"She did. And the part of the advice that I remember was when Ann Landers sort of laid out this rule. She said there were some things, by the time you got to a certain point, that you shouldn't hide."

"To a certain point . . . ?"

"Well, in a relationship."

141

"Oh, okay."

"She said it would be harder to deal with that kind of thing if it came out later."

"Oh, yeah. I've read about situations like that. Some woman marries a guy, and umpteen years later she finds out he's still married to some other woman, and they've got kids, and so forth. Or a guy finds out his wife has been married more times than she told him."

Dusty laughed. "Yeah, or a guy finds out he's been married to a guy all along." She paused for a second and then went on. "But this case wasn't quite that dramatic. And Ann Landers' advice was pretty simple. She just said there were some things you shouldn't hold back on."

"Uh-huh."

"One was whether you'd ever been married, and the other was whether you'd ever had any kids."

Jim felt his eyebrows go up. "I guess so. That's nothin' to lie about, but I suppose some people do." Then a dark thought crossed his mind. "I hope you don't think I've had anything covered up. I mean, you know I've been married before, and I've never had any kids."

"Oh, no. I didn't mean that."

"Hell," he said, "in a town like this, everybody's life is an open book anyway."

"Except for all the little secrets."

He had a vision of a drawn window shade with the silhouette of two people facing each other. "Yeah, I guess there are a lot of those." He had heard stories of girls, young teenage girls, who had run off to get married, and then their parents had chased them down and gotten things annulled. Dusty didn't seem like one of those. He looked at her.

She took a deep breath and said, "Well, I've got one of those little secrets. It's something I'm not proud of, but it's a fact about me."

"Uh-huh."

"When I was just out of high school, I got into a little bit of trouble."

Jim had an idea of what was coming next. Her careful tone of voice, with the selected words, reminded him of how he spoke about himself. It seemed as if she was feeling just as he had felt. "Uh-huh."

"And I had an abortion."

He winced. "That must have been a rough thing to decide."

"It was. And I was pretty mixed up. I didn't know which way to turn. I didn't love the guy, and I was still living at home."

Jim nodded and took a sip of wine. He could think of nothing to say, and he didn't feel as if he had to say anything. The mood of the moment seemed positive, so he let it be.

"You know," she said, "I think if it happened now, I would keep it. But at the time, it didn't seem like an option. It didn't seem possible."

"It's like children having children. You see it, but—"

"But it's not good. Of course there was no good way out, anyway. I just couldn't imagine raising a baby. The only two options I could see were to do the operation or have the baby and give it up."

"That would have been hard, the second one—especially in a small town like this."

"Well, it's been done. A girl just goes away for a while."

Jim reflected. "Yeah, I guess so."

"It happened to an aunt of mine. Not in this town, but it's happened here, too, for that matter. Anyway, she's fifteen years older than I am, so we've talked about some of these things. She told me that when she was about the same age she got into trouble, and she went to one of those homes for unwed mothers. Down in Sacramento. When she had the baby they took it away, and that was it. Of course she wanted to keep it by then, but she had already signed it away, and she had all the family pressure."

Jim let out a breath. "That sounds awfully hard."

"It wasn't anything I wanted to go through. And I was such a mess, I just wanted to get through it as soon as I could."

"I guess any way you would have done it, you would have had bad feelings about it."

"Unless I had kept the baby. But I didn't know that then. I know it now."

Jim realized he had just spoken without really knowing what he was talking about. As a way of not making another stupid comment, he nodded.

"Anyway," she said, "that's my story. It seemed like the type of thing I was supposed to bring out."

Jim found himself nodding again. "I don't suppose it's an easy thing to talk about."

"No, it isn't. But I haven't talked about it with that many people."

Jim was on the verge of assuring her that the secret was safe with him, when he realized that she probably meant something else. She probably meant it was a delicate confidence. "Thanks for feeling that you could tell me," he said, laying his hand on hers.

She had her lips tucked in against her teeth. "Thanks for listening," she said.

Then they turned towards each other, and he put his arm around her waist as they kissed.

The kitchen light seemed to shed a bright glare as they sat at the table with the pear pie between them. The sensation of going from the dark room to a lit room reminded Jim of those times, in adventures of the past, when he and a woman had come out into the cold glare of a living room or kitchen. In one way the present moment was similar, in that he and Dusty had shared some intimacy in the darkness; but in the fuller sense there was no resemblance, because he did not have to look her in the face and cooperate in staring down the embarrassment. There was, really, nothing to feel uneasy about. A story like hers was bound to keep them restrained for a little while longer, he imagined, although it would not have had nearly that effect if they had already been to bed together.

Dusty held a steak knife upright, then lowered it as she used both hands to rotate the pie dish. "You know how it is," she said. "Sometimes you know you've got to tell this story, because you can't keep it trapped inside any more. Then once you tell it, you're done with it."

Jim looked at her. He didn't think she was talking about the same story. "Yeah?"

"It's like one of those stories you have to unload on someone else." Her mood seemed lighter now as she poked the knife through the crust of the pie.

"Well, I'd better let you."

"It has to do with my mom. She said she bought the pears off a truck on the side of the road, and the lady selling the pears was selling T-shirts, too. So my mom bought a T-shirt because she thought I would like it, and she tried to give it to me."

As Jim saw the twinkle in Dusty's eye, he felt a smile come onto his face. "Go ahead."

Dusty pointed at her abdomen. "Well, there was a picture of two pears on the front of the T-shirt, and it read, 'Another fine pear from Lake County.' Spelled p-e-a-r."

"Uh-huh."

"Only there were two."

"Oh, I get it. A pair." Jim pictured two pears, and he imagined what kind of a pair they would suggest on a woman's T-shirt.

She pursed her lips as she cut the second side of a wedge of pie. "She tried to give me the T-shirt. I wouldn't take it."

"Why?"

"I don't like that kind of T-shirt." She gave him a cute smile, almost sexy. "And I wouldn't wear it anyway. I'm not from Lake County."

CHAPTER 14

The next morning, as Jim worked on building a stall for Babe, his thoughts were all on Dusty and her visit the night before. She had gone home shortly after the pie and coffee at midnight, but she had left his senses in a swirl. Although they had both had their reasons for restraint, he knew there was some good old energy at work on both sides.

In retrospect, his response to her story reminded him of the way he would react to learning that a young woman was a single mother. On one hand it confirmed something promising, that she knew which end was up; but on the other hand, it suggested that she had already made her mistake and might be awfully careful about making it again.

Beyond the physical level, the confidence she had shared took on more meaning as he thought about it. Her misgivings about the abortion, and her comments about how she would regard a baby now, struck an agreeable chord in him.

All the time he had been married to Elaine, the "B" word was something they either didn't talk about or agreed to talk about later. As he considered it now, in this new light, he realized it would come as no great surprise if Elaine never had any children. While he conceded to himself that he did not know how she saw herself, he still imagined that she probably did not see herself as a child bearer. Dusty, he imagined, was the opposite, and he interpreted that probability as a good sign. He knew that if he looked for good signs he would find them whether they were real or imagined, but in this case he was convinced that the good sign had presented itself.

As he continued to think about it, another positive aspect occurred to him. In the last few months he had imagined he might end up with a woman who already had a kid or two — maybe even someone who had had her limit and had cut off production. He had been thinking that way because of the general principle of having equal baggage. Somewhere close to the surface he had feared that with someone like Dusty, sooner or later he would be disqualified from continuing a relationship. Now the fear wasn't so strong. He knew the idea of equal baggage didn't fall under any system of weights and measures, and he knew that his sense of baggage was just his sense. Furthermore, he felt that his past outweighed Dusty's. But knowing that she had been through her problem helped him understand why she had seemed more serious or more mature than other young women her age. He thought that perhaps in some undefined way, a sense of intuited balance had helped make things possible between them. There was no undoing their respective mishaps, and he saw that if they accepted the past as it was, they might be able to make some good out of the present and possibly the future.

Another thing he found encouraging about Dusty was her interest in the outdoors. She liked the country, she liked the horse, and she liked to camp. That was a big change from Elaine, who as much as refused to live in the country and who had never roasted a hot dog on a willow stick. Dusty spoke fondly of camping and cook-outs, and she had said she would like to do some of those things she used to do with her father and brother.

More than ever he liked the prospect of their relationship getting somewhere. He felt he had moved through his compulsive period with Arlene, and he didn't have his guts tied up in knots like Claude did. Just being around Claude made him realize how lucky he had been to come through his own divorce and its aftermath as clean as he had. If he had not gotten those earlier things settled he would not

148

have been ready for a relationship with Dusty. He knew that.

The bean plants in the leased ground were turning yellow. Jim had little interest in the crop itself, but now that it was getting close to being harvested, he felt encouraged. There hadn't been much activity in those fields since he had moved in. The hoeing and cultivating had already been taken care of before the plants reached full growth and put on their pods. In the last month, the only activity had been irrigating, and the irrigators had come and gone inconspicuously and then quit coming at all. Now it looked as if harvest wasn't very far away, and he would be done with lease farming, at least for the time being.

On Saturday morning he woke up and looked out the back window to see two large machines cutting beans. By eight in the morning the drivers had finished the field in back and had left the machines down below, where at some point in the middle of the night, when the dew came in, they would cut again. After that would come the raking, which was quick work, and a few days after that the harvester would come through.

Seeing things now from the perspective of a non-farmer, Jim noticed the detached nature of mechanized farm work. When he had first started working for farmers, he did open-field work in the beans, tomatoes, and sugar beets. He remembered what it was like. Back then, a tractor job left him out in the open, exposed to the heat or cold, wind or rain. A fellow would hear the sounds of the fields and any odd sounds of the equipment. He also got to smell the earth, the flowers, the water on a neighboring field, or a fire from miles away. Now, most of the tractors were huge, rubber-tired vehicles with glassed-in cabs, where the operator could enjoy a controlled climate and listen to his favorite music.

Most farmers had their own equipment for working the land, planting, and cultivating, but not all of them had their own harvest equipment. Some of the outfits were custom harvesters — some local, some migrant. Usually the operators would wave from inside their glass chambers, but Jim did not often know who they were — if they were local or just passing through.

He thought the cutters and rakers belonged to the lease farmers, who in turn did not have direct contact with Jim because they had leased the land from the bank before he bought the place. Then when the harvesting crew came, Jim saw a different set of vehicles and faces. One face gave him a start.

As he was driving into town on Friday morning, just as he had pulled onto the paved road from his front entrance, he saw a bean truck slowing down to turn into his place. It was a bob-tail truck with a box bed, the type that moved the crop from the harvesters to the bean mill. The truck was a white, square-nosed International with the sun glinting on the windshield. The driver waved, and as Jim waved back, he recognized the man at the wheel. It was Brant.

Jim let out a breath. He thought the man had gone away, but here he was back again, waving. Jim looked in his mirror. What the hell, he thought. Brant could come and go as he pleased. In a few days the crew would take him to some other farm, and in a few days after that he would be somewhere else in the valley. Meanwhile, the idea of not being totally done with Brant was just something he would have to live with. It was sort of like living in the same town with an ex-wife — a fellow got over it and tried to work on a better idea.

It had been a little over a week since Dusty had come to dinner. Jim had talked to her twice on the phone, and he felt comfortable about the way things were going — comfortable enough to imagine inviting her to go on a hunting trip. The late deer season would be starting in another week, and after checking on regulations and dates, Jim saw that it was at least possible for them to give it a try. He called Dusty that Friday afternoon and asked her if she would like to go, and she said she would have to think about it. Jim told her the opening weekend was still a week away, so they had plenty of time to decide. She called him back about fifteen minutes later and said she would like to go. They agreed to leave early in the day on Friday so they could find a campsite and have everything in order for opening morning. Jim said he would call back in a day or two to work on details.

On Saturday, Jim went to visit Ernie. He told him about the upcoming trip, and Ernie offered to take care of Babe. Jim said he would appreciate that, and then he asked about borrowing a tent.

Ernie said it was fine, that they were through camping for the year. "You ought to take the double sleeping bag, too," he said.

Jim gave him a serious look.

"Really," Ernie said. "They're all clean and everything. Brenda took 'em to the dry cleaners when we got back from that last trip."

Jim had his mouth turned down. "We haven't even been to bed together yet."

Ernie shrugged. "It still gets cold. You should take 'em along anyway. If she wants separate bags, they zip apart."

Jim hesitated. "Well, okay. I'll take 'em along as an extra set."

Ernie smiled. "You don't want to take her up there and then have her get mad because you let her freeze."

Jim smiled back. "No, you're right. So if I've got extra bags, no one'll get cold."

Over the weekend, Jim dug out all the necessary gear, some of which he hadn't used in quite a while, and on Monday he called Dusty to talk about the food. She said she would cook spaghetti, which would be easy to heat for one night or for both, if they had to. Jim said that was fine, and he could work the rest of the menu around that idea. On Wednesday evening he went shopping. He picked up a couple of nice rib-eye steaks along with the cereal, milk, lunch stuff, and other groceries.

Then, as if he had the warning voice of Ernie Denman at his ear, he stopped at the liquor store. Dusty had liked the claret, so he picked out another bottle of that, plus a square bottle for opening up camp, and a twelve-pack of Budweiser in the can. He raised his eyebrows and nodded to himself as he set the items on the counter next to the cash register. He hadn't been drinking much since he had sorted things out and had decided what he wanted to do and what he needed to cool. The whiskey, wine, and beer seemed like a full order, but he imagined some of it would make the trip back home.

At mid-morning on Friday, Jim and Dusty rolled out of town and caught the freeway north. They had agreed to go to the general area where Dusty had gone in years past, which was in the mountains west of Red Bluff. As they traveled they talked about past hunting experiences and about the weekend ahead. They talked about the menu, the hunting they planned to do, what they would do if they got a deer — they talked over just about every detail except the sleeping arrangements.

At the edge of a little town called Platina they stopped and ate lunch on the tailgate. Jim had bought some black rye bread, pastrami, and hot mustard, plus some white cheese that came from a factory in the valley. They drank a beer each as they ate their sandwiches and shared a bag of potato chips.

The sun was warm, but autumn whispered in the air. They had been traveling through foothill and scrub oak country, and the National Forest lay yet ahead of them. When they got into the mountains, the weather would be cooler and the days would end more quickly as the sun dropped behind the peaks.

Once into the mountains, they took a Forest Service road north. It took them through typical National Forest country of timbered mountainsides, clear-cuts, burns, re-planted areas, and huge slash heaps from old logging operations. It was pine and fir country. They came out on a high tableland that seemed to have sparser growth and more stunted timber than the country they had just passed through. It looked interesting, so they decided to find a camping spot.

Among the hunting stories, Jim had told Dusty about Claude wanting to go to Buzzard Roost. She had met Claude when he came into the restaurant after the bars closed, so she had followed the story with a smile. When Jim stopped the pickup at a possible campsite, Dusty said, "It's not Buzzard's Roost, but I guess it'll do."

The smell of the dust and the pines together brought up the feeling of freedom that Jim always felt when he took a trip to the mountains. It was the feeling of being up and away from all the petty stuff, of being at large in a timbered country that rippled away in all directions. The air was cooling already in the late afternoon, and he felt the mild excitement that came with setting up a new camp. The sidewall of the pickup was cooler than it had been at lunch time, but the camp gear was warm and smelled like the valley as they set up the tent and unpacked the furnishings.

He could not help feel humor in the situation as he stood in the tent with Dusty. Here they had come all this way together, were off by themselves in the mountains for two nights, and so far had avoided mentioning the sleeping arrangements. Finally he just smiled and said, "Well, how shall I roll out the beds?"

"I suppose this way," she said, moving her arm in a north-south motion.

"I mean, separate bags or a double bag?"

"It's going to get cold, isn't it?" She seemed to be amused by the moment, also.

"I'd think so," he said. "Probably close to freezing."

"That's a double bag there, isn't it?"

"Yeah."

"Well, let's try it, and we can use the single bags for blankets if we need them."

He yawned and nodded, as if they had just decided to use melmac instead of paper plates. He didn't want to seem too eager, but inside he felt happy, and not just because of the prospects. Whether they arrived at any further intimacy or not, she had made a nice statement of trust.

Once they had the tent in order they organized the camp outside. The site had an old circle of rocks with dirt and charcoal in the middle. Jim cleaned it out and re-shaped it into a firepit. Then he and Dusty went out for firewood so they could have a fire when the sun went down. All the firewood was pine. It broke easily, with several pieces jumping and flipping with the blows of the ax, and after a little while they had an armful each.

Back at the campsite, Jim set up the white gas stove so they could heat the spaghetti. Then with an upside-down wooden crate as their table, they set up drinks to celebrate the ritual of opening camp.

Dusty had a glass of wine, while Jim had bourbon and water. When he didn't have Ernie's standards to live up to, he went with a more modestly priced square bottle, which meant bourbon and white label instead of sour mash and black label. The plastic glasses did not clink when Jim and Dusty touched them together, but it made a fine salute.

The shadows lengthened, and Jim started the fire. When they had been gathering the firewood he was sorry not to find any manzanita, which he had taken a liking to at Uncle

Calvin's ranch. Now that he had the fire going, though, it seemed perfect in its own way. The smell of dry, burning pine added to the general sensation of being in camp, and the glow of the campfire helped define their little place in the surrounding world.

When the spaghetti was warm, Dusty poured each of them a glass of wine. With the crate again as their table, they had their dinner.

After the meal, Jim scooped out fresh ice and mixed another bourbon and water. He and Dusty put on jackets and moved their chairs up to the fire. Dark was drawing in now, and a half moon had lifted above the pine trees to the east of camp. Jim looked at the clear sky and remembered that the hunting was supposed to be better when the moon wasn't full. He hadn't been keeping track, but he thought they should be due for another full moon in less than two weeks. That was all right; he would take whatever moon came along.

Jim turned back to the fire. The pine was making a good blaze, and he found the heat and the smell of the burning wood to be reassuring.

"You know," he said, "being in camp is almost like another life. You go through all the rigmarole to get packed, you drive and drive to get there, and once you're there, it's like you've always been there. Even if you haven't been to that particular spot before."

Dusty nodded. Then after a pause she asked, "Did you ever go camping with your wife?"

Jim shook his head. "No, not at all." Then a thought flashed through. "That double bag is Brenda and Ernie's."

"Oh. I hadn't given that any thought."

"Well, for whatever it's worth, Ernie said it just came back from the cleaners."

Dusty smiled in the firelight. "No cooties, then."

Jim laughed. "No, no cooties."

That night they slept together, Dusty in her pajamas and Jim in his thermal undershirt and flannel boxers. They kissed good-night and rolled over with their backs to one another. Jim wondered if he was going to be able to sleep at all, but before long he was in the world of dreams, where he saw a deer with giant antlers rubbing its tines on the guy ropes of the tent.

CHAPTER 15

In the morning they had breakfast of cold cereal and milk as the coffee perked. When it was ready they had about a cup and a half each as they huddled by the open flame of the gas stove. The moon was gone, and the trees were black shapes in the last darkness of early morning. When the sky began to lighten above the tips of the trees, Jim turned off the stove. He and Dusty shook out their coffee cups and put away their chairs. They took their rifles from the gun rack and got ready to hunt. Jim turned off the lantern and nodded to Dusty, and together they left the dark camp behind them.

That morning they hunted the timber together, moving quietly and talking with signals as much as with words. They saw no deer, but they walked enough country to get an idea of its layout and how they might hunt it that afternoon and the next morning. About a mile below camp, in the direction beyond the point at which they had come in with the pickup, they found a waterhole that had recent deer tracks around it. They crouched together and spoke in low voices.

Dusty said she would like to sit and watch the waterhole that evening. "That's how I shot my first deer," she said. "I know how to sit still and be quiet."

"That's fine. I can go on a long, slow walk to the west here, and stay out of your way."

The day had warmed up pretty well by the time they got back to camp. It was past eleven, so they set their chairs in the shade and brought out lunch materials. The dark bread, white cheese, and pastrami again made the main course. There was no sound of motor vehicles to be heard, and the wind whispered through the needles of the pine trees. A chipmunk perched on a log at the edge of the campsite, and a blue jay squawked from a nearby tree.

"Doesn't take long for them, does it?" Jim said.

"Nope," she said. "That's a good reminder to keep everything packed up."

After lunch they sat for a while in their chairs. "You know," he said, "we really didn't hear very many shots this morning."

"Maybe there aren't very many hunters up here."

"Or deer."

Dusty laughed. "That's all right, if it means fewer hunters."

Agreeing that they might hunt right up until dark, they decided to gather firewood now so they would have it for the evening. They went a little farther out than they had gone the evening before, and in less than an hour they had a suitable stack of firewood in camp.

In the lazy part of the afternoon, they took a siesta in the tent. At straight-up noon the tent was hot, but now the shadows had moved and the inside was comfortable. Jim lay on his back, on top of the bedding, with Dusty not far away. The warm, dry smell of the bedding mixed with the tick of the clock and the occasional rustle of the wind, and Jim savored the sensation. This would be good to remember, he thought — being in camp with good company.

He woke up and saw the shadow of the pines a little longer on the roof of the tent, so he sat up and put on his boots. He unzipped the tent and went outside to sit in a camp chair, where he laced up his boots and let his mind clear. He heard the zipper of the tent and looked around, and he saw Dusty smiling as she came out of the tent.

"About time?" she said as she came near.

"Yeah, I think so."

They went over the plan again after they took their rifles from the gun rack in the cab. Dusty would watch from her spot while Jim would go on a walk, and they would both make it back to camp by dark. Then Jim kissed her on the cheek, told her to shoot a big one, and walked off into the brush and timber, turning once to wave back.

He walked in a slow, steady arc to the west, pausing from time to time to let the sounds gather, and then moving on. The sun was slipping, as he could see from its position in the tree tops as well as from the angle of the shadows. The air temperature was warm but not hot, and it, too, seemed to be dropping. When he came to a spot that he imagined as the far point of his walk, he stopped and sat for a few minutes. He had gotten pretty well warmed up, and when he had sat long enough to cool off, he lifted his rifle from his lap and stood up. Then he heard a shot.

It came from the general direction of the waterhole that Dusty would be watching. The sound carried for a long while, rumbling out through the draws away from him as well as toward him. Jim knew it was a rifle shot, but beyond that he wasn't certain. He turned in the direction of the waterhole and headed that way.

It had an interesting effect, that shot. It brought Dusty to mind, although she hadn't been far from his mind as he had drifted through the brush and the stunted timber. He was pretty sure she was a good shot, so if it was Dusty shooting at a deer, she probably had one down. He smiled. It pleased him to think of her making a good shot.

He remembered what she had looked like as she came out of the tent, with her flowing hair and sparkling eyes. Then he remembered what she had looked like when he had seen her last, in sweatshirt and blue jeans — when he had kissed her on the cheek and told her to shoot a big one. At the edge of the camp she had turned and waved when he did; he remembered that, now.

Now he enjoyed the idea of her poking through the brush, rifle in the crook of her arm as she studied to see if the deer had lost any blood. From what she had said, he was confident she was a good hunter and knew to go check, even if the deer had bolted and stayed on a dead run.

She had told him a story about hunting in the Black Hats with her brother. He had shot at a big four-pointer, and from the way the buck wheeled and ran, Greg was furious and certain he'd missed. Dusty, as she told it, found a fleck of blood in the dirt, and they followed the hoofprints until they saw antlers lying on the ground, sticking out from behind the brush where the buck had dropped.

Maybe she had shot and missed. Still, it pleased him to imagine Dusty, even in her disappointment, making sure. The shot had given him a clear sense of her, a sense of her presence or person. He felt her, thinking and feeling, maybe kicking a rock in disgust because of something she had done.

He stopped. It was the draw, the type of draw that told his mind that a deer might be there. Evening would be coming on, and deer would be out of their beds, mincing and browsing.

He knelt down, with brush in back of him to absorb his silhouette. His gaze wandered, and on the return loop of a figure-eight he saw the doe. She was across the draw headed down, frozen still and looking straight at him. Her mousy color blended in with the dried grass and the grey-green tint of the buckbrush. He knew her for a doe, but he routinely put the scope on her and checked for horns. Then he scoped the draw, and behind the doe he saw a smaller deer, a yearling. After about seven or eight minutes of watching, not ten anyway, he got up. The two deer bounded down the draw, and Jim started walking. It was cooling off now, and he shivered and flexed his shoulder muscles. Then he settled into a steady walk.

Thinking of the shot again, he assured himself that if Dusty had shot, it had been a serious shot. She had said she had learned not to take a bad shot, and from the very little they had hunted together already, he knew that hunting was quiet and serious and fun for her, like it was for him — like he thought it was supposed to be. Hit or miss, it would be good to hear about in camp, over dinner.

He walked at a steady pace, zigzagging through the trees to avoid deadfall and low branches. The afternoon light was fading, but he knew where he was headed, so he did not slow down or pause.

As he walked toward the waterhole, he thought of the possibilities ahead. If she had a deer down, they would be a while taking care of it. They could heat up more spaghetti and have a glass of wine. If there was no deer, they could go ahead and barbecue the steaks as they planned, and they would still have time for conversation and a drink before they crawled into the tent.

It would probably get close to freezing again. This morning when he had shivered out to make the coffee, the ice cubes in his plastic cup had been exactly as they had been the night before when he'd set it down. The temperature had dropped and stayed just so, so that the ice hadn't melted or re-frozen. He remembered that now; the ice cubes were exactly the same.

Now at the waterhole the evening was getting thick, but he could see well enough to see that nothing was out of order. He whistled, short and sharp. No Dusty. Back at the tree she had said she might sit against, he thought he could make out her footprints going back to the camp.

Slinging his rifle over his shoulder, he slipped his thumb into the sling strap and stepped into a direct march, back in the direction she had headed. He knew that up ahead in the trees there was a clearing, where a fire would cast its light on the face of a pretty girl.

Tonight he would lie near her again in the double bag. He would smell woodsmoke in her hair; in the jackets they used for pillows he would smell pine and dust and smoke. He would drift to sleep hearing the even tick of the Big Ben, and beyond that, maybe the wail and yap of the coyotes.

It was a pretty smart uphill march, enough to get him started sweating again. He realized he was thirsty, and getting hungry. In a few minutes he'd find out if it was her shot.

Before he got back to camp he smelled the campfire. Then he saw the camp, light in the darkness that had now set in. He noticed she had put on a sweater, and in the lantern's glow her hair moved as she bent over the pickup tailgate. It looked as if she was cutting up vegetables for a salad. A plastic glass of wine tittered in front of her. The pickup door was open.

He clucked as he stepped into the campsite.

She looked up and smiled. "See anything?"

"Doe and fawn," he said, as he unslung his rifle and poked it into the gun rack. "Did you? I heard a shot."

"No, I didn't see anything."

"Whose shot was it?" Closer now, he saw that the sweater was soft and purple-colored, like the downy new blossom of a bull thistle.

"Two jerks in a Blazer. They took a dumb shot at a jack rabbit. They missed."

"Good." He went to the ice chest and took out a beer, opened it, took a swallow, and came back to stand by her. Her hair lay soft against the magenta sweater.

"They never even saw me," she said. "They must have driven within thirty yards of me. Just drove through."

"Good." He saw the half moon rising above the trees, just as it had done the evening before. It would be another clear evening but not too bright. He put his hand on Dusty's shoulder, and she turned to kiss him. This was a good way to be, he thought — just a man and a woman together, in camp.

162

John D. Nesbitt grew up in the farm and ranch country of northern California, where he worked in the fields for many years as he went through school. He earned a bachelor's degree at UCLA and then a master's and a doctorate at UC Davis. He now lives in the plains country of Wyoming, where he teaches English and Spanish at Eastern Wyoming College in Torrington. Four traditional western novels, *One-Eyed Cowboy Wild, Twin Rivers, Wild Rose of Ruby Canyon,* and *Black Diamond Rendezvous,* have been published in hardbound, large print, and paperback. He has also brought out four short story collections, including *Antelope Sky,* a collection of modern West stories, and *Seasons in the Fields,* a collection of stories about rural California. His first contemporary western novel, *Keep the Wind in Your Face,* was published by Endeavor Books. His fiction, nonfiction, book reviews, and poetry have been widely published. He has won many prizes and awards for his work, including a Wyoming Arts Council literary fellowship for his fiction writing.